GUIDE TO
California Wines

GUIDE TO

California Wines

BY JOHN MELVILLE

NOURSE PUBLISHING COMPANY

San Carlos, California

To the memory

of

Joseph Henry Jackson

who first made this book possible

ACKNOWLEDGMENTS

To: *Dr. A. Dinsmoor Webb,* Associate Professor of Enology, College of Agriculture, University of California, for his kindness in checking Part I of the *Guide* from the enological and viticultural points of view;

the *Wine Advisory Board* for permission to use the California wine map;

the *Wine Institute* for the list of Wineries that are open to the public (Chapter XVII) and other material;

Roy W. Taylor, Public Relations Director, Wine Institute, for his unfailing cooperation;

the *Owners* and/or *Managers* of the various wineries mentioned in the *Guide,* for their cooperation in checking the text concerning them and for supplying much useful information;

my wife, *Willy,* for her sage advice and assistance in getting the work done.

Note: In spite of the help and assistance of the above-mentioned persons and organizations the author remains solely responsible for the text. His aim is to present the material in an accurate manner. Nevertheless errors will undoubtedly have crept in, either of fact or of judgment. He regrets such errors sincerely and invites correspondence to correct them in later editions should this edition prove popular enough to warrant them.

THE AUTHOR

ACKNOWLEDGEMENTS

PREFACE TO THE SECOND EDITION

THIS NEW EDITION of the *Guide to California Wines* makes its appearance due to popular demand. Designed as a practical reference volume for both the trade and the public, its aim is to present the wines of California in a comprehensive, accurate and interesting manner. So little information is available on this fascinating subject in book form. To fill that need is the purpose of this work. It has been completely rewritten and brought up to date. Much new material has been added.

California wines have come of age. Only the uninformed will deny that they have their own and diversified charm. The best of them, actually, match in quality, character and flavor all but the very finest estate bottled wines of France and Germany and are much more reasonable in price. Any host can be proud of serving them, even at the most formal occasion. A wine does not have to be imported to be really good. The savoring of a fine Cabernet Sauvignon or Pinot Noir will readily prove the fact. If the inevitable snob is not to be convinced, remove the label first. Better still, remove the snob!

California produces wines as different as the grapes from which they are produced and, as climate and soil, vary according to region. PART I of this volume describes the various kinds of wines produced, grouped according to their overall type. PART II tells about the more notable wineries producing directly for the public while listing their best known brands. PART III discusses, chartwise, the serving of wine and glasses. Here too will be found a listing of California wines especially recommended because of their outstanding character and a list of wineries that are open to the public. *Bon voyage!*

The author hopes that the reader will derive as much satisfaction from consulting the *Guide* as he had pleasure in composing it. He trusts also that the day is not far off when the United States of America, one of the great wine producing countries of the world, will adopt the serving of a glass or two of wine with the evening meal as a natural and national custom. So enjoyable and healthful a habit will do much to relax the personal tensions of the day and to promote feelings of well being and goodwill.

Casa Carnbee
Carmel-by-the-Sea, California

CONTENTS

Part Three

CALIFORNIA VINES AND WINES

*C*ALIFORNIA WINES are produced from vines imported from Europe or from neighboring regions, and belonging to the famed *Vitis vinifera* species of grapes.

The art of wine making was brought to California by the Spaniards. From Mexico wine growing spread northward to Baja California and finally to what was then known as Alta California. According to tradition, Padre Junipero Serra, of Mission fame, brought the first vines from Baja California and planted them at Mission San Diego in or about 1769. The Franciscan Fathers planted vines near the various Missions they established along their Camino Real stretching northward to Sonoma. The oldest California winery is to be found at Mission San Gabriel, where the famed Trinity Vine, planted around 1775, flourished for over a century and a half. It was from San Gabriel that settlers set forth one day to establish the Pueblo which was to become the city of Los Angeles.

The Mission Fathers planted what became known as the Mission grape, popular for long and still used today, mainly in the production of dessert wines.

The first layman wine grower of record was Governor Pedro Fages, who planted a vineyard along with his orchards in 1783, not far from his residence in Monterey, Alta California. Dona Marcelina Felix Dominguez, the first known woman wine grower of Cali-

fornia, planted, in the early eighteen hundreds, at Montecito near
Santa Barbara, a fabulous vine which was to bear in good years some
four tons of grapes. Known as *La Vieja de la Parra Grande,* or
"The Old Lady of the Grapevine," she was said to be 105 years old
when she died in 1865.

For a time Los Angeles led the rest of California in wine growing.
There Joseph Chapman, an early immigrant, is conceded to have
been the first viticulturist. He is far overshadowed in fame by Jean
Louis Vignes, a native of the Bordeaux region in France and the
possessor of a most appropriate name. By 1843 his celebrated Aliso
Vineyard, in the heart of what is now downtown Los Angeles and
named after a large sycamore which dominated the entrance to his
property, covered over a hundred acres. Don Louis del Aliso, as he
became known, was the first to import choice vines from Europe
and to realize the great future of California wines, produced from
these varieties. Many of his relatives followed him from France, including Pierre Sanssevain, who became a well-known grower in his
own right.

In the northern region the first great wine growing pioneer was
General Mariano Guadalupe Vallejo. Born in Monterey of Castilian
descent he rose to prominence at an early age, becoming closely identified with the Mexican and early American history of California
and especially with that of Sonoma, where he resided for many years.
He was a great gentleman, farmer, soldier and philosopher. He accepted the "manifest destiny" whereby Alta California, in its own
interest and by the force of circumstances, was to become part of the
United States. In June 1846 a company of Americans ran up the
Bear Flag in the plaza of Sonoma and soon afterward the American
Army raised the flag of the United States. Vallejo, in spite of a brief
incarceration by the overly patriotic Bears, accepted the new regime.
He continued to devote himself to his agricultural pursuits and to aid
immigrant Yankees to settle in the newly opened region. He was the
first non-missionary wine grower in the Sonoma Valley and domi-
nated the viticultural scene there for many years, until the advent of
Haraszthy.

Colonel Agoston Haraszthy is often referred to as "the father of California's modern wine industry." It is greatly owing to his genius that a sound and lasting basis was created for the state's viticulture. It is a pleasing thought that the wine growing estate near Sonoma, which Haraszthy called Buena Vista and made famous, is in operation today. It is there that some of the story of this colorful California wine growing pioneer will be found.

California wineries have a long and proud tradition. Many of the better-known enterprises flourishing today were founded in the nineteenth century, some still being run by members of the founding family. Their listing by county and in approximate chronological order, according to the owners' claims, presents an intriguing historical and geographical picture.

In 1849, or earlier, the vineyards in San Benito County now known as Valliant Vineyards were started by Theophile Vaché. In Santa Clara, Almadén, Paul Masson and Martin Ray are the successors to wine making traditions begun in 1852. In the same county Mirassou Vineyards originated a year later, some four years earlier than Buena Vista in Sonoma. The early sixties saw the beginnings of Charles Krug in Napa and of Schramsberg. Dating back to the seventies are Padre in San Bernardino, Beringer Brothers in Napa, and Inglenook in Napa.

In the eighties a galaxy of famous wineries was founded, including Italian Swiss Colony and Korbel in Sonoma, Mt. La Salle (The Christian Brothers) in Napa, Brookside Vineyard Company of Guasti, Cresta Blanca, Wente and Concannon in Alameda, Italian Vineyards Company (I. V. C.) in San Bernardino (now owned by Garrett and Company with their own wine making tradition dating back in the East to 1835), California Wine Association in San Francisco, Digardi in Contra Costa, Petri in San Joaquin, Ruby Hill in Alameda, the Novitiate of Los Gatos in Santa Clara and Bisceglia Brothers in Fresno.

The nineties witnessed the foundings of Roma, now of Fresno, of San Martin in Santa Clara and of Foppiano, in Sonoma. In 1900 the foundations were laid for Beaulieu in Napa.

Since then many other wineries, great and small, have risen to establish noteworthy wine making traditions of their own.

Prohibition dealt a severe blow to American viticulture in general and that of California in particular. It was a senseless attack, as Prohibition has never led the way to moderation and encroaches deeply on man's freedom of judgment. A substantial part of California's vineyard acreage was maintained for the production of wines for sacramental and medicinal purposes and for supplying grapes to home wine makers, as allowed by the dry laws. Other vineyards were turned over to the cultivation of table grapes and to the manufacture of grape juice.

After Repeal the California wine industry was rebuilt on a sound basis with the State Department of Public Health and the federal government becoming joint guardians for the maintenance of standards as to the identity and labeling of wines.

California is responsible for roughly 90 % of the production of all domestic wines consumed in the United States. Aperitif and dessert wines constitute about 75% of the total California wine production, the balance consisting mostly of table wines and of sparkling wines. Of the table wines approximately four fifths are red, including the rosés, and one fifth white.

The climate and soil of California are particularly well suited to the vines of the *Vitis vinifera* family. Beginning with the days of Jean Louis Vignes and of Agoston Haraszthy, practically every variety of these vines has been planted in California, many of them with great success. By the alchemy of local conditions they yield wines which often differ in character from those produced in their original environments. California wines, while often similar or identical in name to European types, should always be considered on their own merits, but comparisons, it seems, are often inevitable.

The same grapes also develop differently in the various regions and climates of California. Maturity is slow in cooler areas; grapes retain more acid and develop less sweetness, while dark grapes attain the maximum coloring matter in their skins. These regions are best suited for the production of dry table wines and of sparkling wines of quality. Under warmer conditions grapes develop less acid and a greater sugar content. Such zones are better adapted to the production of dessert wines.

It is known exactly to which localities each grape variety is best suited or whether its cultivation should be avoided altogether. Such studies and recommendations are among the important functions of the Department of Viticulture and Enology of the University of California's College of Agriculture, which maintains an experiment station at Davis in Yolo County.

Full recognition must be given to a great line of university figures who have wisely guided California's viticulture and are seeking constant improvement. First of that line was the famed Dean Hilgard who was succeeded by Bioletti, or the great Bioletti as he is often referred to. Both have long since passed on, to supervise, it may be hoped, the heavenly vineyards. Their places are ably taken today by such men, professors of viticulture or enology, as Cruess, Winkler, Amerine and Olmo, familiar figures to all members of the wine industry.

Wine growing and wine production are important and fundamental parts of California's agriculture. There are many more farmer-growers than producers. The interests of both should be adequately protected. Wine making is also a business, subject to the hazards of weather and diseases, to fluctuating grape prices, and to high labor costs. It is at the same time an art, requiring the skill, patience, and devotion of experts.

Fine wines are produced from the better wine grapes, but the latter are often sparse yielders. Standard wines are the product of the more heavily yielding vines of lesser quality. Inferior wines are not infrequently made with table grapes.

Wines produced from the finest grapes naturally will command a higher price. For such wines the name on the label of an outstanding wine grower is helpful as a guarantee of quality. If a sound standard quality wine is sought at a lower price, then the name of a volume producer of a nationally distributed brand should be looked for. These wines are advertised widely and provide good value for the money.

California wine growers often produce, bottle and market wines of many different types, growing some grapes themselves and buying the rest from growers in the neighborhood or from other districts. It is customary for a large producer to market a variety of table wines as well as aperitif and dessert wines and often sparkling wines as well. One reason for this custom is that many different varieties of grapes flourish in the same vicinity; vines which are strangers or even rivals in Europe become friendly neighbors in California. Another, and very potent, reason is that it is much more profitable to market a large variety of wines than otherwise. Only a few California wineries produce wines only from grapes grown in their own vineyards. Most of them buy outside grapes as needed and many bottle wines they do not produce themselves in order to complete the selection of wines they want to market. It must be stressed that the fact that a wine is actually produced at a specific winery from home-grown grapes only can never be as important as the quality of the wine itself, backed by the reputation of the winery which either produces or markets it.

Part One

I

CALIFORNIA TABLE WINES

THE TABLE WINES of California can best be classified according to color; red, white or rosé, and as to whether they are *generic* or *varietal*.

By *generic* is meant a wine called after its European prototype which it resembles, more or less. The names are familiar, easy to pronounce and are met with the world over. In California the best known of such table wines are burgundy, claret and chianti in the reds, sauterne, chablis and rhine in the whites, and vin rosé meaning pink wine.

By *varietal* is meant a wine named after a particular *variety of grape,* from which it is principally or exclusively produced and having the easily recognizable taste characteristics of the variety. The best known California varietal red table wines are Cabernet Sauvignon, Zinfandel, Pinot Noir and Gamay. In the whites they are: Sauvignon Blanc and Semillon; Chardonnay, Pinot Blanc and Chenin Blanc; White Riesling, Traminer, Sylvaner and Grey Riesling. In the rosés they are Grenache Rosé, Gamay Rosé and Cabernet Rosé. These are all names to remember if one wishes to serve the more distinctive and finer table wines of California.

In marketing a table wine with a generic name the producer either tries to approximate the European wine type after which it is called or he simply uses the name in response to public demand. The public insists on burgundy and sauterne. The producers, to stay in business, must comply.

The trend towards varietal table wines is increasing as the public becomes more particular as to quality and flavor. The laws are strict and a wine can—or should be—called after a grape *only* if 51% or more of the wine is produced from that grape. A varietal wine should also possess the distinctive color, aroma and flavor of the particular grape. These qualities should be easily recognizable and not only by the experts. There is little point in producing a varietal wine just for the sake of the name.

Some fine California table wines are produced from a careful blending of choice grape varieties, each lending its own character to the final product. The French Bordeaux wines, both red and white, are usually blended in this manner. There is a place in California for blends as well as for the varietals, straight or otherwise.

Vintage years matter less in California than in France and Germany where temperatures, affecting the grape harvests and the resulting wines, vary considerably. Even so, some years in California are more favorable than others and there is a definite trend towards marketing the table wines of exceptionally fine vintages at a higher price. This development must be warmly welcomed as is the tendency towards differentiating between superior table wines that mature in different vats. There is that elusive quality in nature that seeks perfection in all things.

Indication of the vintage on a California wine also serves to identify it to the consumer. Vintage charts would only be of real value if made up by each winery for each type of wine produced, indicating the vineyards of origin. Incidentally, if a vintage is mentioned on the label, the wine must, by law, have been produced 100% in the year indicated.

Which are the finest California table wines?

The answer involves three separate factors: the grapes from

which the wines are made, the district of origin, and the reputation of the wine grower.

The best table wine grapes yield the finest wines. It is therefore useful to be familiar with these grapes after which the finer varietals are named.

The superior table wine grapes flourish the best in the cooler climatic zones, where they grow and mature "the hard way." For that reason the finest California table wines hail from the northern coastal counties, notably in the counties or valleys of *Napa, Sonoma, Livermore, Santa Clara* and *Santa Cruz.*

These are the "appellations of origin" to look for on the label when desiring the best. Any such appellation means, by law, that the wine has been produced from grapes grown and fermented at least 75% in the area designated.

Premium table wines are also produced in other northern sections as in the counties of Mendocino, Solano, Contra Costa, San Benito and in southern Alameda.

Separate mention must be made of the red table wines produced in the Cucamonga district of San Bernardino County in Southern California. Many of these wines carry the *Cucamonga* appellation of origin on the label.

The ultimate guarantee of quality for any wine is the reputation of the grower or producer.

CHART OF THE MORE PROMINENT
CALIFORNIA RED TABLE WINES

Varietals	Generics
CABERNET SAUVIGNON	Claret
PINOT NOIR	Burgundy
GAMAY	
Zinfandel	
Barbera	Chianti
Grignolino	Vino Rosso

II

CALIFORNIA RED TABLE WINES

A. Varietals

CABERNET SAUVIGNON (Ca-berr-nay′ So-vee-nyon′)

THE CABERNET SAUVIGNON, to use its full and proper name, is the premier claret grape of the world. It is mainly responsible for the superb character and flavor of the celebrated château-bottled and other clarets of the Bordeaux region in France.

In California the Cabernet Sauvignon grape can yield, in the northern coastal region, altogether superior wines. Napa, Santa Clara, Santa Cruz and Sonoma counties produce the finest, some of which are great wines anywhere under the sun.

The finest Cabernet Sauvignons are produced from considerably more than the legal minimum of 51% of grapes of that name as the wine will not stand much blending without loss of character. The best have a deep ruby color, an expansive bouquet and a remarkable flavor, easy to recognize and appreciate. When young they possess a dryness and aromatic pungency that smooth out with age to a rich mellowness. A common mistake is to serve them at a temperature cooler than the average room. At room temperature their inherent tartness will dissolve into their rightful soft and mellow flavor.

There is a wide range of Cabernet Sauvignons, depending on the location of the vineyard, the grower, the age, and even the vat in which the wine matured.

When one desires the best "claret type" California can produce, a fine Cabernet Sauvignon is the wine to buy.

Cabernet

A wine, labeled simply Cabernet, can be one of very different things and the term is therefore confusing.

It could be made mainly of Cabernet Sauvignon grapes (see above) and should then properly so have been named.

It could be made principally from the Ruby Cabernet grape (see below) in which case it would better have been labeled by its own name.

It could be made from a blend of various grapes with the Cabernet name. The label may tell the story or it may not.

This writer, for one, is for abolishing the term entirely.

Ruby Cabernet

A fairly new varietal in the red table wine field. Propagated by the Agricultural Experiment Station of the University of California, the vine is a hybrid of the Cabernet Sauvignon and of the Carignane grapes from a cross made in 1936 which first fruited in 1940. Purpose of the cross was to combine the outstanding character of the Cabernet Sauvignon with the productivity of the Carignane in an attempt to combine high quality and yielding ability in the same variety.

The color of Ruby Cabernet is the same as that of its august parent, Cabernet Sauvignon. Its aroma and flavor, though similar, are much less distinguished.

Ruby Cabernet rates as a red table wine of higher than average quality. The wine, varietally produced in a number of northern coastal counties, is to be watched with interest.

ZINFANDEL

The leading red wine grape of California in acreage, production and originality.

Its origin is uncertain. The best known theory was that the vine was first imported to California by Colonel Agoston Haraszthy, who planted these vines at his Buena Vista estate near Sonoma where they flourished and made viticultural history.

Zinfandel varies considerably in quality and character, the best coming from the coastal counties. It can be a wine of peculiar charm, fruity, zestful and aromatic with a raspberry like flavor. It is essentially Californian in type and has the great advantage of being remarkably inexpensive.

If price conscious and still wanting a varietal red table wine, a good Zinfandel is the wine to look for.

PINOT NOIR (Pee'-no Nwahr)

This is the famous grape that yields the finest of the Red Burgundies of France and the "Blanc de noir" wines from which most of the unblended French Champagnes are produced.

In California the Pinot noir grape * produces wines that can be superb in aroma and flavor, harmonious, soft, smooth and velvety. One hundred % Pinot Noir in California is almost always light in the color as the grape does not carry much pigment so blending to darken color is nearly standard practice.

Napa, Santa Clara and Sonoma counties originate the best. The vine, however, is difficult to cultivate and the wine itself is as difficult to produce properly. Availability of the true Pinot Noir wine is limited and wine, so labeled, varies greatly in quality. It can never be cheap if genuine.

If one desires the highest quality California red burgundy type then a truly fine Pinot Noir is the wine to purchase.

GAMAY BEAUJOLAIS (Ga-may' Bo-zho-lay') and GAMAY

The Gamay is the grape that made the Beaujolais wines of France famous and is responsible for their gay and fruity character.

* Pinot Noir is the correct spelling for the *wine* and Pinot noir for the *grape*. This principle applies to all wines and grapes where the name is followed by an adjective.

In California the Gamay produces a light colored, lively and fruity wine with a delicate flavor.

There are many varieties of the Gamay vine, all similar, more or less. Gamay Beaujolais is produced in Santa Clara County while the Napa County variety is always labeled simply as Gamay. Some notable Gamay wine hails from Contra Costa.

It may be noted that Gamay, like Beaujolais in France, is often served at cellar temperature.

Red Pinot (Pinot St. George)

There is no grape by the name of Red Pinot. The term, however, has won limited acceptance as a red table wine, produced from the Pinot St. George grape, the name under which the wine itself should also be known.

Pinot St. George, no relation to the pinot family but a variety from the south of France, produces a wine of its own distinctive charm, soft, fruity and fragrant. It is produced only in the Napa Valley.

BARBERA

A native of Piedmont, Italy, which has done very well in California. The grape yields a big, rugged, fullbodied, richly colored and very pleasant wine with plenty of flavor and tang which yet can be quite soft to the palate. It is characterized by high acidity which it retains very well. Notable Barberas are produced in Sonoma, Napa and Alameda counties.

GRIGNOLINO

Another native of Piedmont producing in California a wine with an original and popular appeal. Its fragrant bouquet is said to remind one of strawberries and its orange-red color is typical and unique. It is sometimes bottled, on account of its light color, as Grignolino Rosé (see page 32). The best known Grignolinos are produced in Cucamonga and in Napa.

Charbono

Also said to originate in Piedmont, this grape produces a deep-colored, soft and heavy bodied wine, hailing from the Napa Valley and from Contra Costa County.

B. GENERICS

RED TABLE WINE

A wine which has become increasingly popular and is often of very good quality, selling in the medium price range. It makes no pretenses and can be produced from a wide variety of grapes. It seems to be taking the place of Claret and is usually of better quality than the latter.

CLARET

Usually a standard quality wine of no particular distinction, although there are exceptions. Claret used to mean any acceptable red table wine, resembling Red Bordeaux more or less and usually less. The term seems to be headed for extinction, its place being taken by Red Table Wine (see above) or Burgundy (see below).

BURGUNDY

The most common appellation today for a generic table wine of no particular varietal distinction. It can be pleasant enough and has superseded what once used to be sold as Claret. The public demands Burgundy and gets it.

California wine, labeled Burgundy, varies greatly in quality, and ranges from poor to very good indeed, notably when produced by the better known growers of the northern coastal counties.

CHIANTI

The wine of this name is usually marketed in raffia or straw-covered, bulb shaped bottles. In California Chianti has become a type of wine, ruby red, fruity, earthy, medium tart and rather full-bodied, the best known of which is produced in Asti, Sonoma County.

Note: The four generics described above actually overlap in color, body and other characteristics, the main differences often being the bottle shapes.

VINO ROSSO

This type of table wine, mellow and slightly sweet, is similar to the homemade table wines produced by many people of Italian origin throughout the country. The commercial wine of this type, quite inexpensive, has won wide acceptance, especially in Italian circles. Many growers produce it, labeling it with various Italian names. The original dryness in the wine is often compensated by the addition of a slight amount of port.

CHART OF THE MORE PROMINENT
CALIFORNIA WHITE TABLE WINES

Varietals	Generics
SEMILLON SAUVIGNON BLANC	Sauterne
CHARDONNAY PINOT BLANC Chenin Blanc Folle Blanche	Chablis
WHITE RIESLING (JOHANNISBERG) TRAMINER SYLVANER GREY RIESLING	Riesling Rhine Wine

III

CALIFORNIA WHITE TABLE WINES

A. VARIETALS

SEMILLON (Sem-me-yon')

ONE OF the finest white wine grapes in the world and responsible, together with the Sauvignon Blanc (see below), for the character of the famous Sauternes and Graves wines of France.

Semillon, when produced by a top flight grower in one of the northern coastal counties, ranks as one of the finest California wines of the Sauternes type. It is golden, medium to fullbodied with a rich flavor and a flowery bouquet and ranges from dry to sweet.

Outstanding Semillon wines are produced in the Livermore Valley and other very good ones originate in Napa and Santa Clara.

SAUVIGNON BLANC (So'-vee-nyon Blon)

The principal grape variety used for the production of the white Graves wine of Bordeaux and also important in that of the French Sauternes. Known in France as the Sauvignon, it is called Sauvignon blanc in California to distinguish it clearly from the Sauvignon vert (see below).

Sauvignon Blanc is a high quality wine with a distinctive aromatic character, fuller in body and heavier than Semillon. Like the latter it ranges from dry to sweet, the best hailing from the Livermore Valley with its gravelly soil.

Sauvignon Vert (So'-vee-nyon Vair)

The grape is widely cultivated and much used in blending and in the production of California Sauterne of average quality.

It is occasionally met with bottled as a varietal type and can be quite pleasing with its dry character and slight muscat flavor.

French Colombard

Another vigorous producer yielding a wine with a high acid content useful for blending in California chablis and rhine wine types. As a varietal wine it is dry, light, tart, pale golden with a neutral flavor.

CHARDONNAY or PINOT CHARDONNAY (Pee'-no Shar'-don-nay)

One of the greatest white wine grapes of all but a sparse yielder. It is celebrated for producing the finest white burgundies and Chablis of France as well as being used for French Champagne.

In the cooler northern coastal counties the grape can yield a distinguished wine, golden, fullbodied and fragrant, flavorful and smooth, reminiscent of still champagne.

The wine is known under both names indicated above which is confusing. It is hoped that a single term will be agreed upon.

When the finest California wine of the white burgundy or chablis type is the object, this is the wine to secure, bottled by an outstanding grower.

PINOT BLANC (Pee'-no Blon)

A grape second only to the Chardonnay in the white burgundy class. It has made an enviable reputation for itself in California where it can yield an elegant wine of distinctive aroma and flavor, smooth and dry, fresh and fruity. Like Chardonnay its favorite California homes are in the Livermore, Napa and Santa Clara valleys.

Some Pinot Blanc is labeled Pinot Blanc Vrai or True Pinot Blanc. This seems unnecessary as the wine is a Pinot Blanc or it isn't. If it isn't, it should be labeled differently.

Pinot Blanc de Noir (Pee'-no Blon de Nwahr)

A rarity and only produced so far by a very few growers. It is a white wine made from the dark grapes of the Pinot noir (see there) by removing the dark skins before fermentation. The principle is not unusual as much of French Champagne is produced from these very grapes.

Pinot Blanc de Noir, nevertheless, is a most unusual wine, the "biggest" California white wine this writer has had the privilege of tasting with a full body and powerful flavor. If one did not know by looking at it that it is a white wine, one would easily think one were drinking a Pinot Noir.

Like Chardonnay and Pinot Noir a Pinot Blanc de Noir is bound to be expensive.

White Pinot

A misnomer as there is no grape by that name and a very confusing term which, it is hoped, is headed for extinction.

Literally, it is of course the translation of Pinot Blanc but if a wine is made from Pinot blanc grapes it should naturally be labeled as Pinot Blanc (see above).

Actually the term won wide acceptance at one time, and still unfortunately does, for a wine, good enough in its own right, made from the Chenin blanc grape (see below).

Chenin Blanc (She-nin Blon)

A wine made from the Chenin blanc or Pineau de la Loire grape famous in France for the white wines of Anjou and Touraine of which the delightful Vouvray is the best known.

In California the Chenin blanc grape has done very well also, notably in Napa County, where it produces a very pleasing light and fruity wine, that varies from dry to quite sweet.

The modern tendency is to bottle the wine under its rightful name, Chenin Blanc. Occasionally it is still marketed as White Pinot (see above).

Folle Blanche (Fol Blonsh)

The grape is one of the principal varieties grown in the Charente district in France for the distillation of cognac. Transplanted to California it has become a much better drinking wine than in its native soil.

The wine has a rather high acid content making it useful for the production of champagne and the better grades of California chablis. It is occasionally met with as a varietal type, notably from the Napa Valley hillsides and is tartly dry, fresh and fruity, clean both to the nose and palate. A nice, light, luncheon wine.

Green Hungarian

The origin of the vine is obscure but is said, as the name implies, to originate in Hungary. It yields a dry wine mostly used in blending. It is, however, varietally produced, hailing both from Napa and Sonoma counties and yielding wines that are quite different in character but with their own individual charm. They are at their best when not served too cold.

WHITE RIESLING or JOHANNISBERG RIESLING (Rees'-ling)

The premier white wine grape of the world, called Riesling in Germany where it is responsible for all the great Rhines and Moselles. It is also extensively cultivated in Alsace, Switzerland, California and elsewhere.

In California the grape is called White Riesling to distinguish it clearly from other varieties with a Riesling name such as Sylvaner or Franken Riesling, Grey Riesling and Emerald Riesling (see below under those names). Properly, the wine should be called White Riesling and is sometimes so labeled but to the confusion of retailers, restaurants and the public many growers label this wine Johannisberg Riesling naming it after some of the finest of all Riesling wines, those produced by Fürst (Prince) von Metternich at Schloss Johannisberg in the Rheingau district of Germany. This custom seems presumptuous as the correct name of White Riesling renders sufficient honor to one of California's truly great wines while trespassing on no foreign glory. Some producers market this wine with the even longer name of Johannisberger Riesling but federal regulations, thank goodness, frown on this practice and the term is bound to disappear in the near future.

White (or Johannisberg) Riesling is a most refreshing wine, with a pronounced fragrance of bouquet and a rich, satisfying flavor. Napa, Santa Clara, Santa Cruz and San Benito counties are best known for its production. Depending on the vineyard, some are lighter, delicate and pale green, others are fuller in body, fruitier and dark golden.

TRAMINER (Tra-mee'-ner) or GEWURZTRAMINER (Gewurts-tra-mee'-ner)

Two names for the same grape, famed in Alsace, France, and known in California as the Red Traminer on account of the red flush on its skin when ripening. The term Gewurztraminer is sometimes also used to denote selected strains of the Traminer grape.

The wines are fragrant and distinctly aromatic with a spicy scent and flavor and are generally rated as the finest rhine wine types of California after the White Rieslings. They are produced in Napa, Santa Clara and Sonoma counties.

SYLVANER or Franken Riesling

The principal rhine wine type grape grown in California. It is known as the Sylvaner in Alsace, France and as the Franken Riesling in some parts of Germany. In California it is known under both names, but more correctly under that of Sylvaner.

The wines are of superior quality, fragrant and fresh with a delicate aroma and flavor. It is bottled as a varietal in Napa, Santa Clara and Sonoma counties, usually under the Sylvaner name but sometimes, presumably to take advantage of the Riesling name but leading to unnecessary confusion, as plain Riesling (see below under the white generics).

GREY RIESLING

The grape, actually the Chauché gris of France and not a Riesling at all, yields in California a soft and pleasing wine with a mild and spicy flavor. It has attained great popularity and the demand often exceeds the supply. The best known Grey Riesling comes from the Livermore Valley but it is also produced in Napa, Santa Clara and Cucamonga.

Emerald Riesling

A hybrid of the White Riesling and the Muscadelle, originated by the University of California at the Agricultural Experiment Station at Davis, Yolo County.

The wine rates as a table wine of above average quality and has a clean, fresh, tart taste. It spoils easily, however, acquiring a brown color and an oxidized flavor.

Veltliner (Velt'-leener)

The Red Veltliner grapes can produce an agreeable white wine, somewhat similar to Traminer (see above). The grapes have a slight pink blush when ripe which explains their name.

The wine has sufficient varietal character to warrant bottling as such. Much wine bottled as Traminer (see above) actually comes from Veltliner grapes as the two are often confused in the vineyards.

Malvasia Bianca (White Malvasia)

The grape is a muscat flavored variety of the Malvasia vines which are said to originate in Greece and are widely grown in Europe. In California it yields a sweet light table wine of delicate bouquet and flavor. It is variously labeled by its full and correct name of Malvasia Bianca and as California Malvasia without indication of color.

The wine should not be confused with the dessert wine of the same name (see page 46) nor with the scarce red Malvasia table and dessert wines.

B. GENERICS

WHITE TABLE WINE

Unassumingly named, California White Table Wine varies from average to very good indeed. It is usually dry. Many white wines, sold under fancier names, regional and other, would do as well if not better were they labeled with this simple and straightforward appellation. It is a matter of educating the public.

SAUTERNE(S), Dry, Medium and Sweet

California Sauterne is usually spelled without the final "s" of French Sauternes. A few growers use the French spelling but the general tendency is to the shorter, Americanized form.

Sauterne is produced in California from a variety of grapes, from the finest to the prolific but neutral tasting Thompson Seedless, which is actually a table grape. It ranges from dry to sweet, from straw to golden in color, while its bouquet and flavor depend on the grapes used.

Haut Sauterne has come to mean a sweet or medium sweet California Sauterne while Chateau Sauterne is reserved for the sweetest type, often made from Semillon and/or Sauvignon blanc grapes, with the addition sometimes of a little Muscadelle, the same grapes from which the best French Sauternes are also produced.

The finest California wines of the Sauternes type, outside of the Chateau wines just mentioned, are the varietal wines known as Semillon and Sauvignon Blanc (see under white varietals).

CHABLIS (Sha-blee')

The generic type of white burgundy named after the famed French wines of that name from the Chablis region.

California Chablis is pale in color, usually more delicate than sauterne and less tart than rhine wine. It is made from a variety of grapes, from fine to indifferent.

Some excellent chablis is produced in the northern coastal counties by outstanding growers. The inexpensive ones are often not to be distinguished from dry sauterne and rhine wines of the same brand.

Rhine Wine

The California wine so labeled is made from a variety of grapes and often from the same as those from which chablis (see above) is derived but blended in such a manner that a paler, drier and tarter wine is obtained.

The best of these wines are the product of one or more of the Riesling grapes (see below) and then possess the aroma, flavor and character of the latter.

Riesling (Rees'-ling)

This wine can be a number of varietals or a blend of some or of all of them. The term has become confusing and in this writer's opinion had better be abolished altogether.

If the wine is a true varietal, made from 51% or more from either the White (Johannisberg) Riesling, the Sylvaner (Franken Riesling), the Grey Riesling or the Emerald Riesling (see under the varietal whites) it should be labeled under one of those names.

It can also be a blend of one or more of these wines without any of them predominating. The result is that California Riesling varies greatly in character and quality, depending on the grapes used, the district or vineyard of origin and the grower. It has, in fact, become a meaningless appellation.

Note: Riesling is often misspelled and mispronounced "Reisling," presumably because of an erroneous impression that it sounds more Germanic.

Hock

Hock is an abbreviation of Hochheimer, a German Rhine Wine at one time very popular in Britain, and became a generic name to denote any wine of the Rhine type. The name is still used in California but is disappearing.

Moselle

This term used to be popular to designate California wine of the Rhine type. It is still occasionally used for table wines but is more familiar in describing sparkling white wines that have been carbonated (see under Sparkling Moselle).

White Chianti

This wine is marketed, like its much more popular red counterpart (see Chianti under the red generics), in raffia or straw covered bulb-shaped bottles. Its production is very limited.

Vino Bianco

A mellow and sweetish white wine, the counterpart of Vino Rosso (see there) and labeled under different Italian names.

Light Muscat

A light wine, produced from muscat grapes, and varying from sweet to very sweet. It is sometimes labeled as California Light Sweet Wine.

Dry Muscat

A dry white wine made from muscat grapes with limited appeal.

May Wine

A white wine, flavored with waldmeister (woodruff) quite popular in Germany, especially in spring time, where it is served cold, in a bowl, with fruit in season. In California it is produced in Acampo and should be better known.

Retsina

A wine of Greek origin, produced in California to a very limited extent and possessing a tang, appealing particularly to those of Greek extraction. The special flavor is due to resin (retsina) being added during fermentation.

CHART OF THE MORE PROMINENT
ROSÉ (PINK) TABLE WINES

Varietals	Generics
GRENACHE ROSÉ GAMAY ROSÉ Cabernet Rosé Zinfandel Rosé Grignolino Rosé Pinot Noir Rosé (a rarity)	Vin Rosé (Pink Wine) Rosé

IV

CALIFORNIA ROSÉ (PINK) TABLE WINES

A. Varietals

GRENACHE ROSÉ (Gre-nash' Ro-zay)

HE GRENACHE is the grape mainly responsible for the well known French rosé wines from the Tavel district in the Valley of the Rhône.

In California the Grenache is best suited to the coolest regions of the northern coastal counties where it yields one of the most typical and best rosé wines of the state. Both dry and semi-sweet types are produced, the former being the finer.

GAMAY ROSÉ

Made from one of the varieties of the Gamay grape, this is an excellent wine, hailing notably from the Napa and Livermore Valleys. It is usually bottled as a varietal but is sometimes labeled simply as Rosé or Vin Rosé (see below under the Generics) or with some special proprietary name dreamed up by the grower.

Cabernet Rosé

The Cabernet Sauvignon grape yields a very good rosé table

wine, bottled sometimes under the varietal name and sometimes under a proprietary label of the grower.

Zinfandel Rosé

Zinfandel is another grape that lends itself well to the production of rosés with a distinctive bouquet and flavor.

Grignolino Rosé

The Grignolino grape yields a light colored red wine in the first place and so with little effort a rosé can be produced from it. It is produced both in the Napa Valley and in the Cucamonga district.

Pinot Noir Rosé

A rare and choice rosé with distinctive character and flavor.

B. GENERICS

Vin Rosé (Pink Wine) or *Rosé*

Wines so labeled are produced from a variety of grapes including those used for the varietals (see above). Lesser grades are simply blends of red and white wines.

While the best and more typical rosé wines are dry, fruity and slightly but pleasantly tart, quite a few are on the sweeter side, containing a certain amount of residual sugar. Some are even quite sweet.

V

TABLE WINES PLUS

 UNDER REGULATIONS that went into effect July first 1959 it became permissible to market table wines containing up to 5 lbs per square inch pressure of carbon dioxide, defining in effect by law the point at which still wines are separated from sparkling wines. Actually wines containing not more than 5 lbs carbon dioxide are not effervescent. It simply allows growers to produce wines under a blanket of carbon dioxide at lower temperatures thereby obtaining more fresh, fruity flavored wines.

How such table wines will be classified when writing about them remains to be seen. Carbonic still wines has been one suggestion. Table wines plus is another.

"Legally they can not be differentiated from their counterparts which do not contain carbon dioxide" the magazine *Wines and Vines* states in its issue of August 1959 and continues: "the label can not state or even intimate that there is some carbon dioxide in the wine; nor can the wine be advertised as containing this gas. Furthermore the brand name is not supposed to give any clue to the fact that the wine has some carbon dioxide . . ."

Whatever the outcome, a few of these "table wines plus" have already been marketed and more undoubtedly will follow.

CHART OF THE MORE PROMINENT
CALIFORNIA SPARKLING WINES

Varietals	Sparkling Wine Type	
Pinot Noir Chardonnay	Champagne *Nature*	really dry
	Brut	fairly dry
	Extra Dry	medium dry
	Sec or *Dry*	to
	Demi Sec	rather sweet
	Doux or *Sweet*	really sweet
	Pink Champagne or Champagne Rosé	medium dry to sweet
	Red Champagne and Sparkling Burgundy	on the dry side on the sweet side
	Sparkling Muscat or Moscato Spumante Moscato Amabile	definitely sweet

VI

CALIFORNIA SPARKLING WINES

THE BEST California champagnes and other sparkling wines are produced according to the French champagne method whereby the secondary fermentation which causes the sparkles takes place in the very bottle containing the wine eventually sold to the consumer. They include California champagne from very dry to sweet, California Pink or Rosé Champagne and California Red Champagne.

The same wines are produced by the faster and less costly method whereby the secondary fermentation occurs in glass lined tanks or vats according to the so-called bulk or Charmat process. The law requires that sparkling wines produced in this manner be designated as "bulk process" on the label.

In both methods discussed above the wines have been fermented naturally to obtain their sparkle. So when the term "naturally fermented" appears on the labeling this only means that their sparkle has not been obtained by artificial means. Wines where the sparkle has been induced by artificial means are known as Carbonated or Effervescent wines and can not be labeled as "Sparkling."

All sparkling wines are expensive due to the high federal tax which is twenty times that on table or still wines, taxing in effect, not so much the wine as the bubbles.

Champagne

The finest California bottle fermented champagnes and other sparkling wines come from the northern coastal counties. Fair ones are produced in Southern California's Cucamonga district. Bulk fermented champagnes of quality are made in these districts as well as in the Great Inland Valley Region.

Pinot noir and Chardonnay, the grapes used to make the great French champagnes, yield the finest California champagnes but other grapes do very well also, such as Semillon, White Riesling, Sylvaner, Folle blanche.

Some, if little, varietal champagne is marketed, indicating on the labeling that it was made from either Pinot noir or Chardonnay grapes.

In California, as elsewhere, a so-called *dosage* or liqueuring is added to the finished wine before inserting the final cork. This *dosage* consists of brandy, wine and sugar, the amount depending on the degree of dryness or sweetness the producer desires to give to his product.

Now it is a peculiar fact that people often like to fool themselves and so it is with champagne. They like to *think* they like a dry champagne but actually they prefer it to be not so dry. That explains why a champagne labeled *Brut* which is, or was, supposed to be very dry indeed, is not really so very dry at all. An *Extra Dry* champagne is a contradiction in itself, for it is often not "dry" at all while champagnes labeled "Sec" or "Dry" are usually on the sweet side! This system works out to satisfaction of both producer and consumer.

The driest type of champagne made, and only to a very small extent in California, is *Nature,* with no dosage added at all. This type is really dry, though if properly made, not harsh or acid, just right. It is also the most difficult to produce.

Brut champagne is the next driest and very popular with "gourmets" and "connoisseurs" who will order no other unless it were the *Nature*. *Extra Dry* is a happy medium that will satisfy most champagne lovers while *Sec* or *Dry, Demi Sec* and *Doux* or *Sweet* lean progressively more to the sweet side and are dessert wines.

The dosage used in the various types will differ slightly according to the producer. Some do not indicate at all on the label what degree of dryness or sweetness their wine possesses. In such cases it is safe to assume that the champagne is in the medium range.

Pink Champagne or Champagne Rosé

A pink sparkling wine, either bottle fermented or produced in bulk fermentation. It is pretty to look at and favored by the ladies. The designation "Oeil de Perdrix" or "Partridge Eye" has sometimes been accorded this wine in California. In France the term refers to the pink tinge champagne sometimes acquires when made exclusively from dark grapes. California champagne made from Pinot noir grapes only will often have this pink hue.

Red Champagne or Champagne Rouge

A name dreamed up by growers who felt that a high quality *bottle fermented* sparkling wine should have a name other than "Sparkling Burgundy" (see below) as the latter is not required by law to indicate on the label whether it is bottle or bulk fermented.

Sparkling Burgundy

Very popular and so very pretty. It is produced from a variety of grapes, is rarely bottle fermented and often on the sweet side.

Sparkling Muscat or Moscato Spumante

A sweet sparkling wine with a distinctive muscat aroma and flavor, usually produced from the Muscat of Alexandria grape.

For the Italian trade this wine is often marketed as Moscato

Spumante or Gran Spumante, names reminiscent of Italy's best known sparkling wine, Asti Spumante.

Moscato Amabile

An effervescent wine, light in alcohol and very delicate, produced in the Napa Valley. The Italian word *amabile* is used to indicate, as in Italy, that the wine is sweet.

Moscato Amabile, owing to its low degree of alcohol, does not "travel well," losing its sparkle easily. It should be kept in the refrigerator and consumed soon after purchase.

Sparkling Malvasia

Made from the Malvasia bianca grape this wine has a delicate muscat character and is on the sweet side.

Carbonated Burgundy and Moselle

Carbonated wines, where the sparkle is introduced by artificial means, can not, by law, be labeled as "Sparkling," as stated before.

Burgundy is the usual name for the red wines of this type and Moselle for the white. They do not compare in quality to the naturally fermented sparkling wines but can be quite good in their own right. They lose their sparkle easily, however.

CHART OF THE MORE PROMINENT CALIFORNIA APERITIF AND DESSERT WINES

Varietals	Generics
Palomino	Sherry (*flor* and regular): Pale Dry and Cocktail (dry) Golden (medium) Cream (sweet)
Tinta Madeira	Port Ruby Port Tawny Port Vintage Port
Muscat Frontignan Aleatico	Muscatel (mostly from Muscat of Alexandria) Black Muscat
	Dry Vermouth Light Dry Vermouth Sweet Vermouth

VII

CALIFORNIA APERITIF AND DESSERT WINES

*T*HESE WINES constitute about 75% of California's wine production. They are sometimes called "dessert wines" and although most of them have a relatively high sugar content there are "dry" types among them as well as all the variations between "dry" and "sweet." In this *Guide* they are grouped together as "Aperitif and Dessert Wines" for the simple reason that even the sweet types are often used as aperitifs before the meal. In fact, in the United States, the term "dessert wine" is really a complete misnomer as very few people actually serve the sweet types with the dessert. They are used between meals, as an evening refreshment or in the afternoon or morning with or without cookies or cake. Or, as stated above, as aperitif wines before the meal. It is nonsense, in this writer's opinion, to ban a sweet sherry or port, or even a muscat, before the meal as an aperitif. Many women, and even men will enjoy such a wine before the meal. Such has been, and still is the custom in many lands of the world. It is only a British custom that Port is traditionally *never* served before the dessert.

Aperitif and dessert wines contain about 20% alcohol per volume as against table wines which average about 12%. The higher alcoholic content is obtained by adding brandy during the fermentation of the wine. The earlier it is added, the sweeter the resulting wine will be. Some aperitif and dessert wines, with a lower alcoholic content than 20%, are produced for sacramental purposes and for certain states with local restrictions. Such wines are labeled with the word "Light" preceding the type, as "Light Sherry," "Light Port."

The appellation of origin and the varietal designation are not nearly as usual with the California aperitif and dessert wines as with the table wine types. With the exception, in some brands, of the Palomino grape in sherry, of the Tinta varieties in port, of Muscat Frontignan and of a few other minor instances, mention of varietal designation is absent. Most of them are also simply labeled as "California" without further indication of origin. This is a pity for just as the northern coastal counties produce the finest table wines, it is the Great Inland Valley Region that is best suited, on account of its warm to hot climate, for the production of aperitif and dessert wines. It is to be hoped that one day the fact that a Sherry or Port from either the Lodi or Fresno district, for instance, will mean as much to the public as a fine varietal table wine hailing from one of the outstanding northern coastal counties.

A. *CALIFORNIA SHERRY*

The main characteristic of sherry, wherever it is produced, is its more or less pronounced *nutty* flavor, and it is to this end that the grower develops his basic wine. Most suitable for its production in California, as in its native Spain, is the Palomino grape, also known in some wine growing districts of California as the Golden Chasselas and it is from this grape that all the finer California sherries are derived. The fact is then often indicated on the label.

California sherries are produced by two entirely different methods. Most of them are treated by the so-called heating or "baking" method, similar to that used for Madeira wines in the island of that name off the coast of West Africa. California *flor* sherries owe their special character to a process resembling that used in Spain for Spanish sherries of the drier types.

In the heating method the basic wine is fermented to the desired degree of dryness, brandy being added to check the fermentation. It is then heated in oak or redwood containers for a number of months up to a year at a temperature of about 120 degrees Fahrenheit. This takes place in heated cellars or by the vats being heated by coils and at times by the warmth of the sun. When the process is completed the wine is gradually cooled and aged for the desired period of time. The oxidation taking place during the heating of the wine gives it the typical character associated with sherry.

In the *flor* process the wines usually undergo primary fermentation by a standard wine yeast to dryness. They are then fortified to ca. 15% alcohol and the growing cells of *Saccharomyces beticus* are placed on the wine's surface. This yeast, covering the wine with a flowerlike crust (hence the term *flor*), lives on the alcohol and other wine constituents and imparts to the wine, by some mysterious alchemy of nature, the characteristic flavor and tang of sherry. The wine, when fully impregnated, is brought up to full alcoholic strength of about 20% and then blended and aged by the so-called "Solera" system.

California wineries have adopted their own Solera systems which vary considerably, resembling to a greater or lesser degree the method by which sherries are aged and blended in Spain. Basically a Solera consists of an arrangement of communicating barrels or vats lying in superimposed rows, four or five tiers high. At periodic intervals the matured sherry is drawn from the bottom row to be bottled, this row being replenished from the row above and so on to the top range which is filled with new wine. In this manner the young wine mixes and ages with the older in one perpetual blend while the Solera itself was started with aged wine in the first place.

Pale Dry or **Cocktail Sherry**

The drier sherries, varying from very pale and very dry to amber and dry. Some producers bottle both a Pale Dry *and* a Cocktail Sherry, the former being usually the paler and the drier of the two.

Sherry or **Golden Sherry**

The medium dry to medium sweet types, golden amber in color. California Sherry, without further indication, falls in this class, as does Amber Sherry.

Sweet Sherry or **Cream Sherry**

The sweet types, usually of a dark amber color.

Note: California *Marsala* is the result of a sherry blend trying to approach the character of the well-known Marsala wines from Sicily, so popular also in cooking. Herb flavored California Marsalas have also been produced.

B. *CALIFORNIA PORT*

Port has been made in California at least since the days of the Gold Rush and is one of the most popular of the socalled "dessert wines." It is often used as an aperitif as well as between meals or after dinner. Conforming to the American taste California port is, on the whole, sweeter and darker than the port wines from Portugal. There is also, oddly enough, hardly any California *dry* port produced.

California port is produced from many different grapes, only a few of which are used for the wine in its native Portugal. To this selected group belong the popular Tinta Madeira, which yields an excellent varietal wine, Tinta Cão (sometimes blended with the former to yield Tinta port), Alvarelhão and Touriga. Another is the Trousseau which has been identified as the Portuguese Bastardo.

California ports are generally sweet, rich, heavy bodied and fruity but often rather bland and neutral in flavor unless produced from the finer and more flavorful grapes. Young port wine, like young sherry, is apt to be "hot" to the taste buds. Older ports, and those where the better brandy has been used in their production, are naturally smoother and mellower. Some will throw a deposit and should be decanted.

Tinta Madeira

A varietal port wine made from the grape of that name and outstanding in character and flavor and fruitiness.

Tinta Port

Produced from one or more of the grapes bearing a Tinta (meaning red) name, such as Tinta Madeira, Tinta Cão. Another very fine wine.

Vintage Port

Derived from grapes harvested in a particular year. Vintage ports are usually fortified with low proof pot still brandy and bottled after one to two years wood age, so that crust may develop in the bottle. Vintage ports should be decanted.

Port and Ruby Port

Most wines labeled simply as port are ruby red and could equally well have been marketed as Ruby Port. There is often little difference, if any, between the two types when produced by the same grower.

Tawny Port

This can be a port that has been aged for considerable time in the wood, the original ruby red color turning to a russet or tawny shade. It can also be a port made from grapes like the Trousseau which naturally yields a wine of a tawny hue.

In the cheaper brands there is often little or no difference between the tawny and other red port types.

White Port

Nothing to do with port at all, this sweet wine is very light in color and neutral in flavor with little, if anything, to recommend it. Sometimes a decolorization process is applied to ensure its light color.

C. *CALIFORNIA MUSCATEL and MUSCAT*

These are among the sweetest of all wines and are of very ancient origin, being mentioned in literature more than 2000 years ago. The great center of California's muscat cultivation lies in the San Joaquin Valley where the grapes attain their maximum sugar content.

Muscat Frontignan

The finest California varietal muscat, delicate, golden and very sweet with a strong muscat perfume and flavor. The name is derived from the French town of Frontignan well known for its muscat wines. The grape is called Muscat Canelli from its original home of Canelli near Asti in Piedmont, Italy, where it is famed for Italian muscat wines, both still and sparkling.

Malvasia Bianca (White Malvasia)

Made from the muscat flavored grape of the same name this varietal wine, containing 20% alcohol, should not be confused with the white table wine of the same name (see there).

There is also a red Malvasia wine, produced in Southern California.

Aleatico

A soft, fruity, aromatic sweet varietal wine, sometimes called Red Muscatel. Some is produced in Southern California. At one time the grape was used to make a table wine of the same name.

Black Muscat

This is a name given to high quality red muscatels produced from Muscat Hamburg grapes or from a blend of these and Aleatico. It is one of California's foremost wines of the "dessert" type and to be recommended also as an appetizer when used with a slice of lemon.

Muscatel

Generally made from the Muscat of Alexandria grape which does so well in the San Joaquin Valley and in the Escondido district in San Diego County.

The wine varies from light to dark amber and from sweet to very sweet. It has a pronounced muscat aroma and flavor if properly made from Muscat of Alexandria grapes for considerably more than the minimum legal percentage of 51%. It is then actually a varietal although this is rarely indicated on the label.

D. *ANGELICA*

Said to have been named after the city of Los Angeles, this is one of the sweetest of all wines. Since California's early days it has been traditionally associated with the Mission grape from which much of the wine is still made. The excessive sweetness is obtained by arresting fermentation at an early stage so the must retains much of its sugar content. Amber in color, it is smooth and liqueurlike without varietal character.

E. *CALIFORNIA TOKAY*

A hybrid wine of little charm unrelated in any way to the re-nowned Tokay wines of Hungary.

California Tokay, amber pink in color, is a blend of angelica or other neutral wine, sherry to give a slight nutty taste, and port to lend it color. Occasionally the Flame Tokay grape, which makes such a brilliant display of its foliage in the autumn around Lodi, is used in the wine's production.

F. *CALIFORNIA VERMOUTH*

Vermouth is named after its most typical flavoring ingredient, wormwood, derived from the woody herb of that name, called *Wermuth* in German. A white wine is used as base while much of the flavoring material is imported. The wine is brought to the desired alcoholic strength and either infused and later filtered or an extract is simply added to it. Besides wormwood a host of other flavorings are used, exactly which depending on the producer and the brand.

There are two main kinds of California Vermouth, the sweet and the dry but the very light and very dry type has won separate recognition. No white *sweet* vermouth is produced, which seems a pity.

Dry Vermouth

This type is also known as French Vermouth as the wine origi-nated and became famous in France. California Dry Vermouth is pale golden or light amber in color and averages about 18% alcohol by volume. It is made with a neutral white wine base of relatively high acid content which is fortified and blended and to which about half an ounce of herb mixture or extract is added per gallon of wine to obtain the desired character.

Light Dry Vermouth (Extra Dry, Very Dry, Triple Dry, Dry White)

A very light and very dry vermouth created to satisfy (it is hoped) advocates of the driest and palest of dry martinis.*

Sweet Vermouth

Also known as Italian Vermouth as it originated in that country. It is reddish amber to brown in color, aromatic, quite sweet and contains about 16% alcohol by volume.

White wine is used as a base to which one to one and a half ounces of herbs are added per gallon to give the wine its desired character. It is then aged in wooden casks but for only a short period of time to prevent loss of aroma through volatilization.

* Happily the craze for ever drier and ever paler martinis seems on the wane so that the danger of a vermouthless martini looms less large than it did some years ago. How straight or nearly straight gin can taste good to anyone remains a mystery to this writer, who fancies himself somewhat of an expert in the art of martini making. Three to four parts of gin to one of dry vermouth seems just about right, depending on the brands used. For the smoothest martinis of all try mixing them the day before, adding a strip of lemon peel and storing them overnight in the refrigerator.

VIII

FLAVORED WINES

$\mathcal{S}$o-called "flavored wines" have made their appearance on the American market in large numbers in the relatively recent past and warrant special notice.

These wines carry proprietary names and generally have a citrus or herb flavoring. They are usually sweet (10 to 14% sugar content) and generally have the same alcoholic content (20%) as the regular types of aperitif and dessert wines.

A flavored wine may be designated legally as an aperitif wine if it contains herbs in a sufficient degree to be detected by a tasting test. Wines that do not contain herbs or that contain herbs in such minute amounts that they are not detectable in such a test may not legally be designated as aperitifs. Hence the term "flavored wines."

Exactly which flavors and herbs are used depends on the individual wine and its producer. Predominant use is made of natural citric flavors, primarily lemon and lime, and of fruit flavors such as blackberry, cherry, loganberry and raspberry. The use of rose, violet, pure vanilla and herb extractions is also indicated.

These wines are sometimes called "natural flavored wines" as the flavoring used in them is natural and not artificial or chemical.

IX

CALIFORNIA FRUIT WINES

A. *BERRY WINES*

*F*RUIT WINES are produced by fermentation from fruit other than grapes. Most of them average around 12% alcohol by volume but a few types are also marketed at 20%, the latter being produced by the addition of spirits or of brandy from the same kind of fruit from which the wine was made.

Berry Wines

California has the largest berry production of any state in the union. All berry wines are fruity and sweet, each with the typical character and more or less pronounced flavor of the particular berry from which it is derived.

Blackberry Wine

The blackberry or bramble is a native of temperate regions and is particularly abundant on the Pacific Coast. There are over 600 named varieties of the blackberry of which the boysenberry (see below) is the best known for wine production in California.

Blackberry wine is produced at both 12% and 20% alcohol by volume.

Blackberry Wine of the Boysenberry Variety

Boysenberries constitute by far the greater part of the black-
berries grown in the United States. They are black when ripe with
a slight blue or purple tinge. The wine they yield has an especially
distinctive aroma and flavor. It is produced both at 12% and at 20%
alcohol by volume.

Elderberry Wine

This wine is made from the umbrella shaped berry clusters of
the American or sweet elder. It is purplish red and has the typical
tangy flavor of the fruit. 12% alcohol by volume.

Loganberry Wine

The berry was named after Judge J. H. Logan who raised it from
seed in his garden at Santa Cruz, California in 1881. The wine is
brilliant red and has a pronounced fruity flavor. 12% alcohol by
volume.

Raspberry Wine

Made from the red raspberry and having the delicate aroma and
flavor of that fruit. 12% alcohol by volume.

Red Currant Wine

Produced from the small tangy berries of the red currant shrub
from which the popular jelly is also made. The wine is light red,
less sweet than other berry wines and contains 12% alcohol by
volume.

Strawberry Wine

California's Santa Clara Valley is famed for its strawberries.
Much of the strawberry wine is also produced there. It is delicate
in flavor and has an alcoholic content of 12% by volume.

B. *FRUIT WINES OTHER THAN BERRY WINES*

Apple Wine

California apple wine is made principally from Gravenstein apples which are specially well suited for the purpose because of their flavor, high sugar content and juiciness. They are grown mainly in the vicinity of Santa Rosa and Sebastopol in Sonoma County. The wine is usually bottled at 20% alcohol by volume.

Cherry Wine

The best cherry wine is made from the sour or pie type cherry which gives the wine a brilliant red color and a pronounced fruity flavor. 12% alcohol by volume.

Peach Wine

A less familiar fruit wine, containing 12% alcohol by volume.

Pear Wine also called Perry

Occasionally met with and containing 12% alcohol by volume.

Part Two

X

NOTABLE WINERIES BY REGION
AND DISTRICT

T HERE ARE two accepted ways of classifying the wine growing districts of California.

The first, as worked out by the viticultural scientists of the University of California, is of primary interest to the growers. The
method is based on the adaptability of the different grape varieties
to the climatic conditions of the various wine growing localities of
the state. These have been grouped, regardless of location, according to the average degrees of heat above 50° Fahrenheit from
April 1 to October 31, and correspond to what can be termed the
cool, moderately cool, intermediate, moderately hot and hot climatic zones.

The type of soil, naturally, also influences the grape as to the
character of the wine it will yield. Even so, the vine draws much
of its nourishment from the surrounding atmosphere, the leaves
of all plants nourishing themselves by breathing in the air.

The second system is the geographical one, which makes it possible to progress from region to region and from district to district
or county. This makes it easy to follow the various wine growing
districts on a map and is the method utilized by this *Guide*.

The geographical system is also preferable for the purpose of this *Guide,* as many wineries obtain grapes, and sometimes wines, from vineyards located in more than one climatic zone, be it from their own vines or from other growers, and either from the same general area or from other districts. Growers in the inland valley often produce table wines from grapes grown in the coastal districts, or blend them with the valley wines, and coastal growers often make aperitif and dessert types from grapes grown in the inland valley areas.

Whether or not a wine has been wholly produced by the grower is indicated on the labeling. The term "produced and bottled" means that a minimum of 75% of the wine has been produced, that is, fermented into wine, by the grower whose name appears on the label. "Made and bottled" means that at least 10% of the wine has actually been produced and that the balance has received some cellar treatment by the grower on the label, although it may not have been produced in his winery. The difference between the two methods of production does not necessarily indicate a graduation in quality among wines, although wineries are naturally the proudest of those wines which they themselves have wholly grown and produced. Wineries which only market the latter are sometimes described as having a chateau operation. Such wines are, or can be designated as "estate bottled."

The more notable wineries of California are presented in the following pages by region and district. In each district they are arranged alphabetically within the locality. Selection has been governed by the quality, both of premium and standard quality wines produced. No prices are indicated, as they will vary according to the part of the country where they are purchased.

A complete listing of all California wineries is published in the "Annual Directory Issue" of the publication *Wines and Vines,**

* 690 Market Street, San Francisco.

while a practical series of Guide Maps, arranged by county, is available at the Wine Institute.*

The California wine producing areas can be grouped geographically in three great regions, as follows:

The cool to moderately cool *northern coastal region,* where all the finest table wines are produced, the top quality champagnes, and some notable aperitif and dessert wines.

The hot *inland valley region,* the home especially of the aperitif and dessert wines, but producing also table wines and bulk fermented champagnes.

The warm *Southern California region,* where aperitif and dessert wines, champagnes, and table wines of note are produced.

* 717 Market Street, San Francisco.

XI

THE NORTHERN COASTAL REGION

*T*HIS REGION, sometimes referred to as that of the northern coastal counties, lies close to the coast north and south of San Francisco and takes in the wine growing districts west of the coastal range of mountains. They are, from north to south:

The *Sonoma-Mendocino, Napa Valley-Solano, Alameda-Contra Costa* and the *Santa Clara-Santa Cruz-San Benito* districts, lying respectively northwest, northeast, southeast and south of the Golden Gate. The city of San Francisco, where a few wineries are located, is treated as a separate district.

A. *SONOMA-MENDOCINO DISTRICT*

This district consists of the two counties which have given it their joint names. Sonoma County yields some premium table wines and champagnes which rate among the finest of the state. It also produces vast quantities of standard quality table wine, mostly red.

Sonoma, with nearly forty bonded wineries, leads all other counties in number. Its wines can conveniently be grouped according to the three valleys where they are produced: the Sonoma, Santa Rosa and Russian River valleys.

SONOMA COUNTY—SONOMA VALLEY

The appellation Sonoma Valley is restricted in the *Guide* to denote the valley proper. The name has often been loosely applied to a larger area, taking in the neighboring Santa Rosa Valley, but the latter is actually part of the Russian River basin and is therefore treated separately. Sonoma Valley is some eleven miles long and is named after Sonoma Creek, which empties in San Pablo Bay to the south.

Sonoma Valley is familiar to many as the Valley of the Moon, made famous in literature by Jack London, who wrote and died there, not far from the ruins of the once famous Kohler winery, destroyed by the great earthquake of 1906.

The Valley of the Moon, or of the Moons, as the Indians used to call it, does its name full justice, for, separated from the Napa Valley to the east by the Mayacamas Range, the moon, to those down below, seems to rise, not once, but many times among the succeeding mountain peaks.

Buena Vista Vineyards, Sonoma

It seems only suitable to begin the presentation of the wineries of California with Buena Vista, once the home of Haraszthy, the "father of modern California viticulture."

Agoston Haraszthy, a man of temperament and of many talents, came from a noble Hungarian family. Because of wanderlust or because he aided in plotting Magyar independence, he left his Hungarian domain and sailed for America. He first settled in Wisconsin, where he founded the town of Haraszthy, which was to become Sauk City. Known as the "Count," he later shed this title for the more democratic one of "Colonel."

In 1849 he came West, to San Diego, which he helped to develop and where he was elected the town's first sheriff. He later represented that county as state assemblyman and moved north to Sacramento. San Francisco, thriving with the Gold Rush, next attracted the colonel's energetic spirit and he became the official melter and refiner of the U.S. Mint. He landed in difficulties, accused of exceeding his legal limit of gold wastage, but was absolved by the court and his name completely cleared.

Haraszthy had been interested in viticulture ever since his early Hungarian days. In California he had planted vineyards near San Diego and in San Francisco near Mission Dolores as well as at Crystal Springs, in what is now San Mateo. He realized, from the example of Jean Louis Vignes at Los Angeles, that the better California wines were produced from European grape varieties and he himself had already imported many such vines, including, as has been widely accepted, the one he named and became known as Zinfandel.

Haraszthy finally chose Sonoma as the ideal place to realize his ambition of establishing the finest vineyards in California. He became a neighbor of the pioneer grower General Vallejo, who produced a wine of great repute, Lachryma Montis, named after his estate. The two families became friendly rivals in wine making, and became much closer than friends when the double wedding took place at the Mission San Francisco de Solano in Sonoma in 1863, uniting Natalia and Jovita, daughters of General Vallejo, to Attila and Arpad Haraszthy, sons of the colonel.

Haraszthy had named his country place Buena Vista because of the sweeping view of the Sonoma Valley and San Francisco Bay and here he constructed an imposing Pompeian mansion. Hundreds of acres of vines were planted and a series of tunnels dug deep in the hillside for cellar accommodation. Skilled viticulturists came to work at Buena Vista, among them Charles Krug, who was himself to become one of California's leading wine growers.

It was at Buena Vista that Haraszthy wrote his classic "Report on Grapes and Wines of California." He advised all growers to test as many varieties as possible, to cultivate those which throve the best and produced the finest wines. He was certain that California could yield "as noble a wine as any country on the face of the globe."

In 1861 Haraszthy was appointed by Governor John G. Downey to report on wine growing in Europe. From a viticultural point of view the trip was a great success. He visited all the important European wine growing districts and collected some 100,000 cuttings from 300 grape varieties, all of which he planted on his return. Financially the journey proved a source of discord. The California Legislature refused to pay the expenses incurred, but the colonel could find consolation in being made president of the California Agricultural Society.

Haraszthy had reached the summit of his prestige. The fame of Buena Vista wines had spread far; offices of the company were operating in San Francisco, Chicago, New York, Philadelphia and London. In October 1864 Colonel and Mrs. Haraszthy were hosts at a Vintage Ball and Masquerade, the social event of the time.

Then financial and other troubles succeeded each other rapidly. Phylloxera struck, Haraszthy suffered losses on the Stock Exchange, taxes on spirits wiped out his profit on brandy, a fire raged at Buena Vista, ruining much of the wine, credit was cut off from the bank, and financial assistance from other sources proved unavailable.

So the "father of California's modern wine industry" left Buena Vista, Sonoma, and California for good. He went to Nicaragua, where he obtained a government contract for the distillation of spirits from sugar and there he started a new domain. But one day, in July 1869, he vanished. It is believed that he tried to cross an alligator infested stream by means of an overhanging branch which broke off by his weight and plunged him to his doom. The life of a great American pioneer had come to a tragic end.

In California Attila and Arpad Haraszthy continued the family wine making tradition. Arpad became famous for his "Eclipse" Champagne, while Attila stayed on at Buena Vista to fight the phylloxera, which was not conquered till the turn of the century. The estate suffered a further great blow when the 1906 earthquake brought down in ruins much of the winery and caved in the storage tunnels, burying, so it is believed, much champagne beneath the debris. Buena Vista entered a dormant period in wine making which lasted till 1943.

In that year Frank H. Bartholomew, now president of the United Press International (U.P.I.), acquired a large acreage of the former Buena Vista vineyards and revived the society, restoring also the two stone wineries from Haraszthy's days.

The following premium wines are available under the *Buena Vista* label:

Table wines:
  RED: Cabernet Sauvignon (Estate Bottled), Pinot Noir, Zinfandel (from the vineyards where the wine grew to fame), Burgundy;
  WHITE: Pinot Chardonnay (Estate Bottled), White Riesling Johannisberger (Estate Bottled), Traminer (Estate Bottled, Vintage), Sylvaner (Estate Bottled, Vintage), Sonoma Semillon (Vintage), Green Hungarian (a *Buena Vista* specialty), Chablis, Vine Brook (from *Franken Riesling* grapes, Vintage), Grey Riesling (Estate Bottled);
  ROSÉ: Rose Brook (from Cabernet Sauvignon grapes, Estate Bottled) and Grenache Rosé;
Champagne (Bottle fermented): Pinot Chardonnay Champagne (Brut, Estate grown);
Aperitif or Dessert Wines: Ultra Dry Sherry and Vintage Port (both finished in small oak casks).

Hanzell Vineyards, Sonoma

The reason for the existence of the beautiful Hanzell Vineyards high in the hills behind Sonoma overlooking the romantic Valley of the Moon is simple but inspiring.

After returning home from Italy where he had served as Chief of the Marshall Plan from 1948 to 1950 the well known business man, financier and diplomat J. D. Zellerbach and Mrs. Zellerbach bought a country place in the Sonoma Valley. Highly appreciative of fine wines the thought came naturally to establish vineyards on the hillsides sloping down from the house. A perfectionist and partial to the great burgundies of France, Mr. Zellerbach had his vineyards of some 16 acres planted exclusively to Pinot noir and Chardonnay, responsible for the glories of his favorite Romanée Conti and Montrachet. From that developed the idea of building a model winery and making his own wine, the finest California could produce. It was to be an operation in the grand manner and great traditions. Experts, including sages of the University of California, were consulted in the layout of the vineyards and in equipping the winery. No effort was spared in securing the best of everything. Winery equipment was specially designed at great expense, glass lined stainless steel tanks of the most modern type were installed, small oak cooperage was imported from Nuits St. Georges in Burgundy, an up to date and efficient laboratory was provided. Appropriately the winery was named Hanzell Vineyards, a contraction of Hana, as Mrs. Zellerbach is called, and of the family name.

The policy of Hanzell Vineyards is to approach perfection as closely as possible. The winery is still in the experimental stage. Much research work is being done by the winery's chemist and *Maître de Chai,* R. Bradford (Brad) Webb.

The first crush took place in 1956, consisting of one barrel of Pinot Noir and five barrels of Chardonnay. No wines will be marketed unless they have reached full maturity and are worthy of the *Hanzell Vineyards* label.

Samuele Sebastiani, Sonoma

This winery, one of the largest producers in Sonoma County and the oldest wine enterprise in the Sonoma Valley operated continuously by one family, was founded in 1904 by Samuele Sebastiani who immigrated from Italy at an early age. From a small beginning—the 501 gallon tank he purchased from the old Bullotti Winery and which still is in use today—he gradually built up his enterprise through hard work, a strong determination to succeed and a deep faith in spiritual assistance.

During the 40 years that Samuele Sebastiani was a prominent figure in the Sonoma wine industry his operation grew to be Northern California's largest individually owned winery with a cooperage of one and three quarters million gallons. He shared his success with many about him, building homes for his workers and donating a parochial school. For the people of Sonoma he built streets for the town, an apartment house, a theatre, an auto court, recreational facilities and completed many other projects.

When Samuele Sebastiani retired his son August took over, putting much energy into wine making, distillation processes and improvements in general. His father, however, never failed to visit the winery until his death in 1944.

Some vineyards are owned in the Sonoma Valley but most of the wines are produced from grapes purchased year after year from the same growers. The winery's operation was mostly on a bulk wine basis supplying other wineries and bottlers throughout the nation when August Sebastiani decided in 1954 to enter the field of premium wines. Much money went into research while the know-how and experience were already present. To get the full flavor of the Sebastiani enterprise let us quote August Sebastiani, owner and general manager:

"We inherit that peculiarly favorable grape soil of Sonoma, a bountiful sky of rain and sunshine, and a people willing to work and to take great pride in their product. We are proud of what we produce."

There is no doubt that August Sebastiani is a man who inherits the love of wine making from his father and who possesses the industrial skill of an organizer with modern ideas based on old but dynamic and proven methods. He believes that there is nothing S S wines can't accomplish. A charming host and a dedicated person he lives with his closely knit family on a hilltop right in Sonoma not far from his beloved winery. Many medals in the winery's sampling room testify to the family ability in wine making.

The featured brand is S S, used for table wines, aperitif and dessert wines including vermouths, and (bottle fermented) sparkling wines. August Sebastiani is particularly and justly proud of his *S S* Barbera, a hearty, ruby red and smooth wine made from the Barbera grape. Other featured wines are the *S S* Chablis, Riesling and Pale Dry Cocktail Sherry.

SONOMA COUNTY—SANTA ROSA VALLEY

The Santa Rosa Creek, after which the valley is named, empties its waters eventually in the Russian River. The city of Santa Rosa is where the Luther Burbank home is to be found. The famed botanist and horticulturist, who was also greatly interested in viticulture, lies buried beneath the cedar of Lebanon in the city park.

Martini & Prati Wines, Inc., Santa Rosa

Some eight miles northwest of Santa Rosa, near Forestville, lies the extensive Martini and Prati Vine Hill winery, operated by Elmo Martini * and Edward Prati.

The Martini family have been in the wine business in Santa Rosa since the eighteen seventies. Raphaele Martini bought the present winery and vineyards shortly after the turn of the century, the enterprise being expanded at various times and later operated by his sons. In 1943 the property was purchased by the Hiram Walker interests, owners of W. A. Taylor and Company, but in 1950 the winery and vineyards reverted back to Elmo Martini, in partnership with Enrico Prati of Italian Swiss Colony fame and with the latter's son Edward. Enrico Prati passed away in 1952 and Elmo Martini is now president of the company, while Edward Prati, who also owns vineyards of his own, is secretary-treasurer.

The winery is the second largest in Sonoma County. The featured brands are *Martini & Prati* and *Fountaingrove,* the latter label having been purchased from the owner of Fountaingrove Ranch, once a famed winery.

* Not to be confused with Louis Martini of St. Helena, Napa County.

Santa Rosa Winery, Santa Rosa

A small winery and family concern, owned and operated by C. B. Meda, born in San Francisco of Italian parentage. He learned the art of wine making from his father, who came from Piedmont, near Asti, and was in the wine business in Connecticut since 1893. On the latter's retirement the son took over the enterprise until the advent of Prohibition.

After Repeal C. B. Meda purchased the Santa Rosa winery, his main interest being to produce fine table wines and especially champagne.

Sparkling wines (bottle-fermented) are the winery's specialties. They are highly rated and include *Brut, Extra Dry* and *Demi Sec* Champagne, from Pinot Chardonnay and other selected grapes, as well as Sparkling Burgundy, from Pinot noir and other varieties. They are marketed under the *Grand Prize* brand, as are the winery's *table wines,* which include Chardonnay.

SONOMA COUNTY—RUSSIAN RIVER VALLEY

The Russian River finds its source in Mendocino County and flows south into Sonoma, turning west past Healdsburg to empty in the Pacific Ocean some ten miles beyond Guerneville.

The lower Russian River Valley, around Guerneville, forms a small, separate wine growing area, where some of the finest California champagne is produced. The inland or upper section of the valley takes in the area around Healdsburg northwards to Cloverdale and on into Mendocino County.

F. Korbel & Brothers, Inc., Guerneville

The great, castle-like Korbel winery, standing among vineyards and huge tree stumps, is situated on the bank of the Russian River a few miles east of Guerneville, just beyond Rio Nido. It is the home of champagnes that rate among the finest of California and are known throughout the nation and beyond.

It was founded by the Korbels, a story of enterprise dating back to the days of the pioneers.

The Korbel brothers, Francis, Anton and Joseph, were born in the little town of Behine in Bohemia, now part of Czecho-Slovakia. They emigrated to the United States and came to San Francisco in the early eighteen sixties. Ironworkers and machinists by trade they soon found employment in machine shops. Francis, the eldest, built a cigar box factory, aided by his brothers, and such was the beginning of a family enterprise that led by stages to lithography, lumber, the building of a sawmill on the Russian River and finally to the production of wine and champagne.

When all the virgin timber had been cut—the vast stumps of which remain an impressive sight today—the Korbels sought the advice of the University of California on what to raise on the newly cleared land. After a dairy venture that proved unsuccessful vines were planted with the purpose of selling the grapes to Sonoma wineries. When the first crop was harvested grape prices proved to be so low that the Korbels decided to crush the grapes themselves and so they landed in the wine business.

The original winery still stands and in 1886 the first section of the present winery was constructed from lumber and brick made on the property. Table wines were produced at first but in the nineties it was decided to make champagne as well and the latter became the sole business of Korbel Brothers after the second World War.

In early 1954 the Korbel family, headed by Anton and Leo Korbel, sold the corporation to the Heck brothers, another dynasty of wine makers. Adolf L. Heck is president of the company and the champagne producer, Paul R. is executive vice president, taking care of the 1300 acre ranch and of the initial wine production while Ben A. Heck is in charge of sales.

The grandfather of the Heck brothers started the family wine business by owning and operating a small winery in Alsace-Lorraine, at that time part of Germany. His son, Adolf Heck, the father of the Heck brothers, knew about wine making from an early age, and came to this country shortly after the turn of the century, going into the wine business in Chicago. In 1933, with the advent of Repeal, the family moved to St. Louis where Adolf Heck senior took over the operation of the American Wine Company, producers at that time of Cook's Imperial Champagne. He remained president and general manager until his death in 1946. The American Wine Company having been acquired by the Schenley interests, the Heck brothers went with National Distillers, remaining in the wine business at Italian Swiss Colony. In 1954 the opportunity arose to buy the Korbel winery, something the Heck brothers had been waiting for. And so the name of Heck became identified with that of Korbel in the field of premium wine making.

Quality is the Heck brothers philosophy. They do not believe in making the public drink what they think it should have but rather in giving the public what it wants and making it as well as possible.

The three most important varietal grapes raised at the ranch for the production of sparkling wines are Pinot noir, Pinot blanc and Sauvignon blanc. Some White Riesling and Sylvaner are also grown.

Under the ownership of the Heck brothers bottle fermented Champagnes continue to be featured, made by the original French Champagne process. They are marketed under the *Korbel* brand, as follows:

Korbel Nature (very dry, made especially for gourmets), Korbel Brut (dry), Korbel Extra Dry (medium dry, originally marketed for the Eastern market only but now also available in the West in limited quantities), Korbel Sec (medium dry), Korbel Rouge (red champagne or sparkling burgundy, on the dry side) and Korbel Rosé (a pink champagne marketed in a transparent bottle, delicately sweet).

The Heck brothers have added a light Brandy to the *Korbel* products and since November 1959 have entered the aperitif and dessert wine field by marketing high quality California Sherries (Cocktail Dry and Medium) and California Port, also under the *Korbel* brand.

In 1954 the Heck brothers purchased the Santa Nella Winery

located nearby with the purpose of meeting the needs for future expansion. This winery is used for the production of a limited amount of table wines sold only at the winery and also for that of the *Korbel* aperitif and dessert wines. The brands used for the sale of the wines at the Santa Nella Winery are *Santa Nella* and *Heck Bros.*

L. Foppiano Wine Company, Healdsburg

The winery dates back to the early eighteen eighties and was known as the Smith winery when the late Louis Foppiano, the father and namesake of the present owner, purchased it in 1898. The company is strictly a family concern.

Louis Foppiano was born right on the property, in the building which now houses the company's offices. Raised in the business since his earliest days, he has built it into a prosperous concern, being quite active also in the East.

Table wines are the specialty but the usual types of aperitif or dessert wines are also marketed. *Foppiano* is the main brand with *Sonoma Gold* selling in the East.

Notable is the Vintage Burgundy, bottled under the *Foppiano* label. It is made from Zinfandel and Petite Sirah grapes and is only produced in years when the grapes contain extra sugar, as in 1953 and 1958.

Italian Swiss Colony, Asti

The origin of Italian Swiss Colony is in great part the story of Andrea Sbarboro, who came to San Francisco from Italy in the early eighteen fifties as a youngster to work in his brother's grocery store. Twenty years later, by working hard and saving, he bought his own store and turned builder and financier.

In 1881 he founded the Italian Swiss Agricultural Colony with the purpose of aiding Italian and Swiss immigrants to settle in their new land. Many of these were vineyardists by trade and a 1500 acre tract was chosen in Sonoma County, suitable for the planting of vines. The land was named Asti after the town of that name in Piedmont, Italy. Each immigrant was provided with room, board, and wages, in return for which a contribution was expected toward building up an equity in the land and eventually becoming an independent farmer. The immigrants objected to the last condition; they were willing to work, but not to take a chance. Sbarboro decided to operate Asti privately. He set the immigrants to work, planting vines with the idea of growing and selling grapes. The price of the latter soon dropped below the cost of production. It was then decided to press the grapes into wine. The first crush was a disaster owing to carelessness in handling; the wine turned to vinegar.

Asti, so far, had proved a failure, but Sbarboro did not give up. He put Pietro Rossi, a San Francisco druggist who had studied wine making in Italy, in charge of the winery. This was in 1888. The first wines Rossi produced were of good quality but the market price offered for them was unprofitable. The Colony then decided to market its wines direct and set up agencies throughout the country and abroad. Italian Swiss Colony finally came into its own. The fame of its wines soon spread and many medals were received in the United States and Europe and even in the original Asti, in Piedmont.

Sbarboro built a sumptuous mansion at Asti and, being a great practical joker, equipped the gardens with a sprinkler system, copied after the one at Hellbrun in Salzburg. The purpose was not so much to sprinkle his plants, but his guests. The grounds of the estate became a maze of booby traps for the unsuspecting.

With the death of Pietro Rossi, thrown from his horse in 1911, one of the great figures of the Colony passed away. Management of the winery was taken over by his twin sons, Edmund and Robert Rossi, who had been taught the art of wine making by their father. Andrea Sbarboro, who among his other duties headed the Italian-American Bank in San Francisco, remained in charge of the Colony's promotion.

Prohibition was the last enemy to strike at Italian Swiss Colony. Sbarboro proclaimed endlessly that Prohibition was not the road to temperance and appeared before Congress in Washington to protest against this threat to man's liberty of action. But he realized that he was fighting a losing battle. He retired from the wine business and in 1923 he died, partly out of disgust, it is said, that his beloved Asti was bottling grape juice. It was, however, by selling grapes and grape juice that Asti was kept going during Prohibition. When Repeal came, the Rossi twins lost no time in reviving the Colony's wine industry and within a few years Italian Swiss had once again become one of the country's leading wineries.

The "experiment that nearly failed" was finally crowned with solid success. During the second World War Italian Swiss Colony was sold to National Distillers Products Corporation who owned it until April 1953 when it was purchased for a record figure by the Petri family, already well established in the wine industry. The next year the Petris also acquired from National Distillers the popular *Lejon* and *Hartley* Brandy labels and several months later the *Lejon* Vermouth brands. Under the Petri direction *Italian Swiss Colony* and its allied brands continued to grow and expand.

Today the *Italian Swiss Colony* labels, together with the *Petri* brands (see Petri Wineries, Escalon) are owned by Allied Grape Growers, a grower-owned cooperative, under the presidency of Louis A. Petri. Allied is said to account for over 25% of the U.S. wine industry volume and consists of about 1200 grape growers throughout California. Assets are said to be over forty million dollars and sales over fifty million. It is also the first time that growers are taking an active part in the sales of wines, being at one and the same time growers, producers and marketers.

Italian Swiss Colony largely produces and markets medium priced wines of good quality but also sells a limited supply of premium wines under the *Asti* label, including aperitif and dessert wines as well as table wines among which there is a Pinot Noir and a Riesling. Generic wines of high quality are also sold by Italian Swiss Colony under the *Tipo* brand. The *Tipo* red and white

Chianti are familiar to many, in their straw-covered, flask-shaped bottles, as is the Grenache Rosé.

The usual table and aperitif and dessert wines are marketed under the *Gold Medal Reserve* and *Private Stock* labels, the latter being slightly higher in price and also used for the (bulk fermented) Champagne and Sparkling Burgundy. In addition there are specialties such as "Cappella," a Vino Rosso type, and *Italian Swiss Colony* Vin Rosé, a popular rosé on the sweet side.

The well known *Lejon* * Vermouths, both dry and sweet, are now produced by Italian Swiss Colony, as are the *G. & D.*† Vermouths. These two brands, it is claimed, dominate the vermouth market in the United States. *Lejon* Dry Vermouth, as the author knows by experience, certainly makes an excellent dry martini.

"Silver Satin" and "Arriba" are both flavored aperitif wines, and "Paree" is a light carbonic still wine (see p. 33).

Italian Swiss Colony did much for what has become a popular pastime for the public, the touring of a winery. It is said that over 125,000 people a year now visit the Italian Swiss Colony's comfortable and attractive tasting room at Asti and tour the winery buildings. Near the ivy covered winery is the original El Carmelo Chapel built by vineyard workers in the shape of a huge wine keg.

Hollis M. Black Winery, Cloverdale

This property, picturesquely situated on the Russian River, was originally the Hall Ranch with a winery that was founded in 1905. Lewis Black and his son Hollis purchased the property from the Halls in 1919, Hollis Black now operating the family enterprise.

The ranch had been in the bulk wine business for some forty years when it was decided, for economic reasons, to concentrate on the production and marketing of premium table wines. To this end the ranch was planted with those grape varieties best suited to Sonoma County. In addition to the home grown wines a number

---

* Named after Lee Jones, a famed figure in the wine industry.
† A contraction of Gambarelli & Davitto.

of other table wines are carefully selected and aged and bottled at the winery.

Varietal table wines available include Cabernet Sauvignon, Pinot Noir and Zinfandel; White Pinot (Chenin Blanc), Sylvaner and Riesling. A Pale Dry Sherry and a Port are also aged and bottled.

All wines are marketed under the *Hollis Black* brand, the label being artistically outstanding and the work of Mrs. Hollis Black, a portrait painter and commercial artist of more than local repute.

MENDOCINO COUNTY

Parducci Wine Cellars, Ukiah

This winery, California's northernmost wine cellars, is located north of Ukiah and is owned and operated by three generations of the Parducci family. More than half a century of wine making experience has gone into the growing success of this enterprise.

While the Parduccis originated in Lucca, Italy, Adolph B. Parducci was born in Santa Clara County. As a youngster, however, he went back to the land of his forefathers where he worked in the vineyards, returning to this country at the age of seventeen. In 1916 he founded the Parducci Wine Cellars near Cloverdale in Sonoma County but later, wishing for more space, he moved northwards to Mendocino County finding the suitable location he had been seeking near Ukiah. Here he established his vineyards and in 1931 began construction of the present Parducci Wine Cellars. The winery, surrounded by vineyards, is located in a charming little valley just off the Redwood Highway.

Adolph B. Parducci is assisted in the family wine business by his sons of whom John A. is the vice president of the firm as well as being the wine maker and chemist. George E. is the office manager while a third generation of Parduccis is becoming increasingly active.

The usual generic table wines are produced but in recent years the accent has been increasingly placed on the dry varietals. These include Barbera, Cabernet, Pinot Noir in the reds and French

Colombard and Riesling in the whites. Bottle fermented sparkling wines are also featured, including Champagne both *Brut* and *Extra Dry,* Pink or Rosé Champagne and the inevitable Sparkling Burgundy. Aperitif and dessert wines, including dry and sweet vermouth, are available for the retail trade.

Parducci is the brand used for all wines of premium quality.

B. *NAPA VALLEY—SOLANO DISTRICT*

This famous district is formed by the two counties bearing those names, with Napa yielding some of the finest of all California table wines.

From a viticultural point of view Napa County and Napa Valley are interchangeable terms, for it is from the valley and its bordering hillsides that the county's famed wines originate. Only the Mayacamas Mountains separate Napa Valley from that of Sonoma, which it parallels. Napa possesses its own romantic name, for in the Indian language it is said to mean "plenty." Napa is indeed the "Valley of Plenty," one of abundant beauty and fertility. Even in ancient times wild grapes are said to have grown here in profusion.

The Napa River which flows through the valley empties, like its Sonoma neighbor, into the waters of San Pablo Bay, connecting with that of San Francisco. Dominating the valley to the north thrones Mt. St. Helena, christened after that saint by the Princess Helena Gagarin, wife of the one-time Russian Governor of Siberia and of the Russian Northern Pacific Colonies and daughter of the Czar of all the Russias.

Napa County—Upper Napa Valley
Schramsberg Vineyard Co., Calistoga

This is the successor to the vineyards and winery of Jacob Schram, made famous in literature by Robert Louis Stevenson.

Jacob Schram (or Schramm, as he first spelled it) was a German barber from Johannisberg on the Rhine who did very well in his trade. In 1862 he bought the Mt. Diamond property on the steep hillsides just south of Calistoga, built himself a winery and a mansion, and had a number of cellars dug deep in the mountain. His Schramsberg wines became celebrated, not only in California, but in far-off places and are said to have been served at the Carlton Club in London.

The Robert Louis Stevensons, while honeymooning on nearby Mt. St. Helena, visited the Schrams and Stevenson related his impressions in the chapter entitled "Napa Wine" of his *Silverado Squatters*. Fanny Stevenson was entertained by the opulent Mrs. Schram on the veranda of the big house, decorated with a wondrous collection of stuffed birds, while Stevenson and his host tasted one wine after the other in the hillside cellars. He tasted them all, Red Schramsberger and White, Burgundy Schramsberger and Schramsberger Hock. There were varietal wines also and Stevenson dwells on the bouquet of Schramsberger Golden Chasselas. The charm of these wines must have been as great as that of their names, which roll so savorously over the tongue.

After Jacob Schram's death the property was inherited by his son Herman. Prohibition rendered Schramsberg useless for wine making and it was sold to a firm of investment speculators. In 1921 it was acquired by Captain Raymond C. Naylor,* who used it as a summer home, and in 1940 Schramsberg was purchased by John Gargano, who had started his California Champagne Company in the early thirties. Gargano had great plans for Schramsberg, but was not able to carry them out because of illness, and he passed away in the beginning of 1952. In 1951 the Schramsberg property was purchased by Douglas Pringle who revived the *Schramsberg* label.

Beringer Brothers, Inc., St. Helena

This famous winery, known also as the Los Hermanos Vineyards, has been continuously operated as a family concern ever since its

---

* Father-in-law of John Daniel Jr. of Inglenook Vineyard Co. (See there.)

founding in 1876 by the brothers Frederick and Jacob L. Beringer.

Jacob Beringer had learned the art of wine making in his native Rheingau in Germany as well as in France and when he came to this country his one ambition was to establish a winery and vineyards of his own, such as he had known in Europe. He found the ideal location for his purpose while on a visit to St. Helena and he persuaded his brother Frederick who was already settled in New York in business, to come out to California and join him in his project. The result was the founding of the Beringer Brothers' vineyards and winery and of a great name in the California wine industry.

The "Los Hermanos" name was aptly bestowed on the firm by a close friend of the Beringer brothers, Señor Tiburcio Parrott, a Spanish gentleman of the old school who lived in a beautiful villa in St. Helena and was a well known patron of the arts.

A special feature of the winery is the maze of tunnels cut into the limestone hill behind it. There are a thousand feet of this tunneling, originally cut out by Chinese coolies with picks. The tunnels provide an ideal storage space at a steady air conditioned temperature for the aging of wines in fine old casks of oak.

Beringer Bros. was incorporated in 1914 with the descendants of Jacob and Frederick Beringer as members. Charles Tiburcio Beringer, for many years president of the firm, died in 1954. Miss Bertha Beringer who wrote a history of the winery and clearly remembers "the elegant carriage driven by a resplendent coachman in which Señor Tiburcio and his lovely wife used to dash up the Beringer driveway to call at the winery" is president. Miss Martha Beringer, Mrs. Olga Beringer and Mrs. Agnes Beringer Young are officials of the company while Otto Beringer, Jr. is the general manager.

Los Hermanos carries on as of old, but adapting itself to the changing times. While the Beringer policy is to market well aged wines blended so their character and quality remain continuous over the years plans are to concentrate more on the production of varietal table wines. Some 305 acres of bare land were purchased to grow the finer varietals.

The featured brand is *Beringer* "Private Stock." Table wines include the regular generic types of which the Sauternes and the Burgundy are the most popular. Barenblut (Blood of the Bear) is a specialty of the house and is a Pinot Noir blend. Varietals include Cabernet Sauvignon, Grignolino, Pinot Noir and Zinfandel in the reds and Johannisberg Riesling in the whites. Cabernet and Riesling are also produced.

The usual types of aperitif and dessert wines are marketed, a specialty being Malvasia Bianca, a wine not often met with at 20% alcohol by volume.

Other products featured are the (carbonated) Sparkler Moselle and Sparkler Burgundy not to forget the well known Beringer Bros. Brandy.

L. Brendel, St. Helena

A small winery and vineyard owned and operated by one man, Leon Brendel. Only one wine is produced, a Grignolino, marketed, appropriately enough, under the *Only One* brand. It is made for 100% from Grignolino grapes and is available both as a red table wine and as a rosé.

Leon Brendel was born at Equisheim, near Colmar in Alsace, France, and comes of a family of wine growers who also made only one wine, in their case Traminer. He studied chemistry at Besançon and Rouffach in France and at Aschaffenburg in Bavaria. With Dr. Goettler he helped to organize a school for distillers in Basel, Switzerland. He went to Mexico at the request of the family of President Madero and became the wine maker and chemist for the Madero winery and vineyards at Parras, Coahuila, Mexico.

At the time of repeal, Brendel came to Southern California, where he established himself as a chemist, wine consultant and wine maker. In 1949 he purchased his present winery where he has been located ever since.

The Christian Brothers' Champagne Cellars, St. Helena
(See The Christian Brothers, Napa)

Hanns Kornell Cellars, St. Helena

Hanns Kornell, a hard working and determined personality, represents the third generation of a family known in Germany since 1848 for their superior wines and champagnes. He attended agricultural college and worked in vineyards and wineries, acquiring experience in France and Italy as well as in his native country. With him as with every true vintner one can say that wine has always run in his blood.

When political conditions made it impossible for Hanns Kornell to remain in Germany he chose America as his new home. In 1940 he hitchhiked to California with $2.00 in his pocket but with determination in his heart. He worked at Fountaingrove in Santa Rosa, then a famous vineyard and winery. He also worked for the Gibson Wine Company in Cincinnati, Ohio, and for the American Wine Company in St. Louis, Missouri, at that time producers of the well known Cook's Champagne, where he was the wine maker and later became production manager.

His great ambition was to manage his own winery and this he accomplished in 1952 when he leased a winery in Sonoma from the Sonoma Wine Company, renaming it Hanns Kornell Cellars. By hard work and a strong inner drive he made his venture a success, so much so that in 1958 he was able to purchase the famous old Larkmead Winery in St. Helena from Italian Swiss Colony. He had come a long way in eighteen years, from two dollars to being the proud owner of his own winery. 1958 was very special for Hanns Kornell for in that year also he married Marylouise Rossini whose grandfather had homesteaded in St. Helena.

While table wines, including Cabernet and Riesling, and aperitif and dessert wines are avalaible under the *Kornell Cellars* the winery's accent is on the production of bottle fermented sparkling wines. These are carefully made, aged and bottled under Hanns

Kornell's personal and untiring supervision. They include *Brut,
Extra Dry, Sec,* Pink (Rosé) Champagne as well as Sparkling Burgundy, all marketed under the *Hanns Kornell* "Third Generation"
brand. Of these the *Brut* Champagne is particularly outstanding.

Charles Krug Winery (C. Mondavi & Sons), St. Helena

This firm, now run by the brothers Robert and Peter Mondavi,
is the worthy successor to Charles Krug, a great figure in the development of the California wine industry.

Charles Krug was born in Trendelburg, Prussia, in 1825 and emigrated to America as a young man. He returned to his fatherland
to take part in the democratic uprising of 1848 and on the failure of
that movement returned to the United States for good. He came
to California and devoted his energies to a study of viticulture with
the aim of establishing his own winery and vineyards. He worked
for General Vallejo and Colonel Haraszthy and became convinced
of the desirability of planting European grape varieties. In 1858 he
purchased some acreage of his own and made viticultural history
by producing, from the grapes of John Patchett of Napa, some 1200
gallons of wine with a small cider press. This was the first wine
obtained in Napa County by modern methods. The press is pre-
served at the Krug Ranch today, a treasured memento of its
founder.

Krug built his original winery at St. Helena in 1861. The fame
of his wines spread throughout the country and beyond. By 1880
the Krug Ranch was considered one of the most beautiful and pro-
ductive in the Napa Valley and Krug himself was well established
as a leader of the wine industry. Such men as Carl Wente and the
Beringer brothers worked for him and obtained valuable experience.

After the death of Charles Krug in 1894 the Ranch was purchased by his close friend and admirer, James K. Moffitt, who used
it as a country home. The winery and vineyards were leased until
Prohibition forced them into a dormant period.

When Repeal came the Moffitt family was willing to sell the
Ranch but only to a wine making family capable of reviving the

fame and prestige of the Krug wines. With a feeling of accomplishing this purpose the property was sold, in 1943, to Cesare Mondavi and his sons Robert and Peter, the present owners.

Cesare Mondavi came to America from Ancona, Italy and his, too, is the story of successful enterprise. He first went to work in the ore mines of Minnesota. There he was chosen by a group of Italian home wine makers to select and buy grapes for them in California. He came to stay, engaging in the wine-grape shipping business expanding later to include other fruit. After Repeal he entered the wine making field, first producing dessert type wines at the Acampo Winery in Lodi (see there). Later he began to produce dry table wines at the Sunny St. Helena Winery in St. Helena. Anxious to concentrate on the production of premium wines the Mondavi family found in the Krug Ranch the means to achieve their goal. Having built up the business with the help of his sons to the present renewed fame of the Krug wines Cesare passed on to his final reward in 1959 at the age of 76.

The Krug winery remains in good hands. Cesare's son Robert, the general manager, and Peter, in charge of wine making have been familiar with the problems and successes of producing and marketing wine since their early years. They both graduated from Stanford University, Robert being later tutored in viticulture by a Professor of the University of California while Peter transferred to this University to take the Enology course.

Since 1943 the Mondavis have renovated the Krug plant at great expense, modernizing the winery and cellars and re-equipping the buildings. In the vineyards the older vines were gradually replaced and always with the finer varietals. In 1958 a new glass-lined tank and bottling room were added. These glass-lined tanks, in essence huge bottles, can hold approximately 125,000 gallons of wine. The purpose is to be able to bottle the wines when they have received the necessary wood age. It has always been the opinion of the Mondavis that just as much damage can be done to the wine if it is allowed to remain in the wood too long as there would be if it were taken out too soon.

In addition to the glass-lined tanks a new method of bottling has been instituted with certain technical advantages making for better wines. Both these innovations are big steps forward insuring maximum quality.

While the name of Charles Krug has been revived to its honored place in the California wine industry his name and that of the Mondavis are interchangeable today.

The main accent of the Krug-Mondavi production is on premium table wines although a few aperitif and dessert wines, including a Tinta Madeira Port, are matured and bottled at the winery to round out the line.

Charles Krug remains the featured brand* for the premium wines. The usual generic table wines are produced; the list of the varietals follows:

RED: Cabernet Sauvignon, Gamay, Pinot Noir and Mountain Zinfandel;

WHITE: Dry Semillon, Sweet Semillon, Sweet Sauvignon Blanc, White Pinot (from 70–75% Chenin blanc and 30–25% Pinot blanc grapes) on the sweet side, Chenin Blanc (from 100% Chenin blanc grapes) on the dry side, Pinot Chardonnay, Traminer, Sylvaner, Grey Riesling and Johannisberger Riesling.

The winery also produces a Riesling and a Vin Rosé (from the Gamay grape).

The Mondavis publish an informative and popular quarterly "Uncorked and poured from time to time by Charles Krug Winery" entitled *Bottles and Bins,* Francis L. Gould, Editor. It gives news about the winery, about the wine industry in general and supplies some very useful and tasty recipes. In 1960 it started on its twelfth year of publication.

Louis M. Martini, St. Helena

The wines produced by Louis Martini rate among the finest of California. Born in Pietra Ligure on the Italian Riviera, Louis M.

' No connection with the Krug Champagne of France.

Martini came to San Francisco as a boy and first assisted his father, Agostino Martini, in the latter's mussels, clams and fish business. In 1906, the year of the earthquake, the decision was made to enter the wine making field. A small plant was built in San Francisco, some forty by seventy-five feet, the modest forerunner of the modern and imposing Louis Martini winery in St. Helena of today.

Louis Martini returned to Italy to study wine making and then returned to California to practice the knowledge he had acquired. He worked for various wine makers, including the famous Secundo Guasti, founder of the Italian Vineyard Company at Guasti (see Garrett & Company, Inc.). Later Louis Martini acquired a plant of his own at Fresno for the making of grape juice and then built a winery and distillery at Kingsburg in southern San Joaquin Valley for the production of sweet wines and brandy. His ambition, however, had always been directed toward producing premium quality table wines. When he sold his Kingsburg plant for a good price he settled in St. Helena to fulfill his ambition, armed with the necessary know-how, drive and capital.

The St. Helena winery was built in 1933 and Louis Martini successively acquired three vineyard complexes. The Villa del Rey or St. Helena vineyard is located on light, well drained soil along the Mayacamas foothills near St. Helena and is planted mainly to Cabernet Sauvignon, Napa Valley Gamay and Chenin blanc (for the White Pinot). The Napa, or La Loma vineyard, part of the former Rancho Rincon de los Carneros, lies on the rolling, gravelly slopes of the southern end of the Mayacamas range, southwest of the town of Napa. It specializes in Cabernet Sauvignon, Pinot noir and Zinfandel vines.

Most famous, however, is the vineyard formerly called Goldstein, planted in the early eighteen eighties and by Martini renamed Monte Rosso after its red volcanic soil. It is situated at an altitude of over 1000 feet on the crest of the Mayacamas mountains dividing Napa and Sonoma counties. In this cool climate wine grape varieties attain top quality. The Monte Rosso vines include Cabernet

Sauvignon, Barbera, Zinfandel in the reds and White Riesling, Gewurztraminer, Sylvaner, Chardonnay, Folle blanche and Semillon in the whites. The wines produced from these grapes are truly "Mountain Wines" and usually carry that designation on the label.

Louis M. Martini, a colorful, vital and forceful figure, is president of the corporation, being ably assisted in the family enterprise by his son Louis P. Martini, the vice president.

Wines are marketed under the *Louis M. Martini* brand and include the following varietal table wines:

RED: Cabernet Sauvignon (Vintage) available in especially fine years as Cabernet Sauvignon Special Selection, Mountain Pinot Noir (available also in magnums), Mountain Barbera (Vintage), Mountain Zinfandel (Vintage), Napa Cabernet (a blend of Cabernet Sauvignon wines of various vintages and lighter in body and color than the wine labeled Cabernet Sauvignon);

WHITE: Johannisberg Riesling (Vintage, from White Riesling grapes), Mountain Gewurztraminer (Vintage, very limited in quantity), Mountain Sylvaner (Vintage, from the Franken Riesling or Sylvaner grape), Napa White Pinot (Vintage, from the Chenin blanc grape), Mountain Folle Blanche (Vintage), Mountain Dry Semillon (Vintage);

ROSÉ: Napa Gamay Rosé (from the Napa Valley Gamay grape).

Generic table wines are also produced: Mountain Red Wine, Mountain Claret, Mountain Chianti and Napa Burgundy in the reds and Mountain White Wine, Mountain Rhine Wine, Mountain Chablis and Mountain Dry Sauternes in the whites. A specialty is the red wine labeled Monte Rosso, a well aged vintage light red wine marketed in the traditional straw covered *fiaschi* and "affectionately named" after the Sonoma vineyard from which it comes.

Four aperitif and dessert wines are available: Pale Dry Sherry (very pale and very dry, of the *Fino* type and aged according to the Solera system), Tawny Port (limited quantity only), Port (ruby red and sweet), Muscatel.

Not generally known is that Louis Martini also produces an

effervescent wine, Moscato Amabile, made from the Muscat of Alexandria grape, light, delicate and quite sweet. It can only be obtained directly from the winery and should be stored in the refrigerator and consumed early to avoid spoiling.

Also available only from the winery direct are small quantities of very special vintage table wines, the vintages varying naturally as time progresses. This gourmet listing of Martini's "Special Wines and Older Vintages" will read: Cabernet Sauvignon (Monte Rosso Vineyard), Cabernet Sauvignon (La Loma Vineyard), Pinot Noir (La Loma Vineyard), Zinfandel (Monte Rosso Vineyard), Barbera (La Loma Vineyard), Johannisberg Riesling (Monte Rosso Vineyard), Pinot Chardonnay (Monte Rosso Vineyard), Gewurztraminer (Monte Rosso Vineyard). In each case the vintage year is indicated as well as the year in which the wine was bottled.

Stony Hill Vineyard, St. Helena

Some seven hundred feet above the floor of the Napa Valley, on the steep hillsides between Spring and Diamond mountains, lies the Stony Hill Vineyard, the name of which speaks for itself. The vineyard, some 30 acres, is planted mainly to three varieties, all white: Chardonnay, Pinot blanc and White Riesling. A small planting of Gewurztraminer has recently been made.

Frederick H. McCrea, vice president and manager of the San Francisco office of McCann-Erickson, Inc., an internationally known advertising agency, for long had the ambition to see what he could do about producing good wines in small quantities. He purchased the Stony Hill property in 1943 and built a small but modern winery in 1951. Crushing of the grapes is done by hand power and the wine is fermented in fifty-gallon barrels.

Production is limited to a small output. Pinot Chardonnay and Johannisberger Riesling are bottled under the *Stony Hill* brand, carrying the vintage on the label as well as the Napa Valley appellation of origin.

Souverain Cellars, St. Helena

It is on the slopes of Howell Mountain, overlooking the Upper Napa Valley from the East that the ranch and vineyards of J. Leland (Lee) Stewart are to be found.

It was in 1943 that Lee Stewart, always appreciative of fine wines, decided to enter the wine growing and wine making fields himself. Headed for Ukiah, Mendocino County, he happened to detour by way of St. Helena and falling in love with the area he found himself purchasing the old Peter Stark place above the Silverado Trail. Gradually he modernized and enlarged the winery and replanted the vineyards. His aim is to combine the best traditions of the European wine grower with the most modern California methods and in this he has handsomely succeeded. An artistic feature of the winery is the beautifully carved entrance door depicting a vintage scene, the work of Merrill Abbott.

What had first started out as a hobby soon became a steady business, running in the black after much work and overcoming many difficulties. The accent is on the production of premium table wines for which Cabernet Sauvignon, Grenache and Zinfandel are grown on the Howell Mountain property. Surplus varietal grapes are taken in from Fred McCrea's Stony Hill Vineyard (see there) across the valley while other varietals are purchased from the Draper Vineyards on Spring Mountain. A close friendship exists between Lee Stewart and Jerry Draper who owns some hundred acres of choice vines and the old La Perla winery which he uses as a summer home. Although he does not produce wine himself Jerry Draper has done a great deal to promote the growing of the finer varietals.

Recently Lee Stewart has made many further improvements to the winery. The storage space has been considerably enlarged, there is now a complete laboratory and office, a refrigeration unit has been added for cold fermentation as well as a new fermentation room including a press imported from Germany.

Bottle fermented champagnes, both *Brut* (from Chardonnay grapes) and Rosé (from Grenache), are produced at the winery and *Los Amigos* Sherry Sack* and Tinta Madeira Port are marketed but the winery's main business is concerned with its premium varietal table wines all from the Napa Valley as indicated on the labeling. Marketed under the *Souverain* brand these include:

RED: Cabernet Sauvignon, Mountain Zinfandel;

WHITE: Johannisberger Riesling (White Riesling), Sylvaner (Franken Riesling), White Pinot (Chenin Blanc), Green Hungarian (a specialty);

ROSÉ: Grenache Rosé

The *Souverain* Burgundy is a blend of Gamay, Zinfandel and Petite Sirah.

Beaulieu Vineyard, Rutherford

A true California chateau with a name for its wines as great as it is justified.

It was just before the turn of the century that a young Frenchman, Georges de Latour, came to California, desirous of producing table wines comparable in quality and character to the finer ones of his native France. He had heard much about California's favorable climate and soil and he came to see for himself. He stemmed from a family well known in both the Bordeaux and Burgundy regions and was already familiar with many of the problems of viticulture and of the difficult art of wine making. He was, besides, gifted with an exceptionally fine taster's palate, an attribute of primary importance to all those engaged in the wine business, and especially in the producing end of it.

Georges de Latour traveled through California searching for the ideal location suited to his purpose and found what he sought in the Rutherford area in the Napa Valley. It was here, in 1900, that he founded the Beaulieu † estate and vineyards, as he named them

* Once produced by Los Amigos Vineyards of Mission San Jose, now no longer in existence.

† Meaning Beautiful Place.

so appropriately. Beaulieu, enlarged and modernized at various times, has remained in the family's hands ever since and is today one of the show places of the valley.

For some forty years Georges de Latour devoted his energies to the production of the finest wines the favored climate and soil of the Napa Valley were capable of yielding. He proved himself eminently successful in his endeavor and established a solid reputation for the Beaulieu wines throughout the United States and abroad.

During Prohibition the winery continued to operate, producing sacramental wines, to which a part of the Beaulieu industry is still actively devoted. Beaulieu is one of the few wineries in California where the accent in wines and wine production is very distinctly inspired by the French taste; the whole atmosphere is that of *"la belle France,"* completely at home in the Napa Valley.

After the death of Georges de Latour in 1940, Madame de Latour presided over Beaulieu in her husband's place. Known to so many for her grace and charm, she had become the *"grande dame"* of California viticulture. With her demise, in 1951, another great figure had passed on.

Today Beaulieu is owned by the daughter of its founders, Hélène de Pins, who, together with her husband, the Marquis de Pins, continues the great tradition set by the De Latours. The Marquis de Pins is a landed proprietor in France; he has a thorough knowledge of fine vintages throughout the world and is known in this country and in France as an outstanding connoisseur and judge of wines. The De Pins divide their time between Beaulieu and San Francisco, and periodically visit France, often touring the various French wine growing districts. Their daughter Dagmar, a wine expert in her own right, is married to a prominent San Francisco real estate investor, Walter H. Sullivan Jr., and Beaulieu's distinguished heritage will continue through them and their children.

The reputation of Beaulieu's wines has progressed with the times, their quality the result of a happy blending between the traditional subtleties of French taste and know-how in the modern California manner. To this philosophy fully subscribes French-trained André Tchelistcheff, who joined Beaulieu in 1938 and is the production manager in charge of the winery and vineyards. He skillfully adapts New World techniques of quality-wine production to his store of Old World wine making experience.

There are four Beaulieu vineyards, two of them located at Rutherford and the other two at Oakville, each being planted with the grape varieties best suited to its particular soil and location.

The brand name under which all wines are marketed is *Beaulieu Vineyard*. As some have difficulty in pronouncing the name, the labels also carry the letters *B V,* and it is by this name that the wines are also widely known. All table wines are labeled with the Napa Valley appellation of origin and with the exception of the Grenache Rosé are estate bottled. The back label indicates exactly from which grapes the wine has been made, the varietals being mostly 100%.

The *Beaulieu (B V)* table wines include:

RED: Cabernet Sauvignon and Cabernet Sauvignon Private Reserve (with extra years of bottle age), Beaumont Pinot Noir, Burgundy (from Gamay, Pinot noir, Petite Sirah and Mondeuse of Savoy grapes);

WHITE: Chateau Beaulieu (from Sauvignon blanc grapes with a touch of Muscadelle du Bordelais), Beaufort Pinot Chardonnay, Beauclair Johannisberg Riesling (White Riesling), Dry Sauternes (from Semillon and Sauvignon blanc grapes), Sweet Sauternes (from Semillon, Sauvignon blanc and a touch of Muscadelle du Bordelais), Chablis (from Chenin blanc, Melon de Bourgogne and French Colombard grapes), Riesling (from Franken Riesling or Sylvaner grapes);

ROSÉ: Beaurosé (from Cabernet Sauvignon, Gamay and Mondeuse grapes), Grenache Rosé (from that grape only).

In recent years Beaulieu has started to produce and market sparkling wines, all bottle fermented. These are the *Beaulieu (B V)* Champagnes, *Brut* and *Extra Dry* and the *Rouge* or Sparkling Burgundy. The year 1960 saw the launching of the *Beaulieu (B V)*

Champagne Rosé (from 100% Pinot noir grapes) in honor of the sixtieth anniversary of the founding of the winery.

Beaulieu also markets aperitif and dessert wines matured in small oak casks including the *B V* Sherries (Pale Dry, regular, medium dry, and Cream), *B V* Port and *B V* Muscatel (from the Muscat de Frontignan grapes).

Most of the varietal table wines of Beaulieu and their sparkling wines carry the vintage year on the labeling and many an older *B V* vintage table wine has become a connoisseur's item.

Inglenook Vineyard Company, Rutherford

The great vinecovered stone winery of Inglenook, home of famed vintage table wines, lies in Rutherford, right in the heart of the Napa Valley. Beaulieu (see there) is its immediate neighbor.

Founder of Inglenook was that colorful Finnish seafarer, fur trader and wine grower, Captain Niebaum.

Gustave Ferdinand Nybom (later Americanized to Niebaum) was born in Helsinki, Finland, in 1842, at that time under Russian domination. He went to sea as a boy and received his master's papers when only nineteen. Two years later he had his own command and in 1864 sailed for Alaska, then also part of the Russian Empire.

For three years he ranged Alaska, the Aleutian Chain of Islands and the Asiatic shore as far as Kamchatka, bartering for furs and acquainting himself thoroughly with the region. Negotiations by the United States for the purchase of Alaska had been started and Captain Niebaum realized that America would have economic as well as political interests in the territory. He made full use of his opportunities and amassed a vast collection of seal skins and other valuable furs. When the sale of Alaska to the United States became an accomplished fact in March 1867 Captain Niebaum lost no time in loading his precious furs aboard a ship bound for San Francisco. He was no more than twenty six when he sailed through the Golden Gate, the owner of a cargo worth well over half a million dollars.

Captain Niebaum's knowledge of the seal habitat was invaluable to the Alaska Commercial Company, organized to obtain exclusive fur sealing rights in the Alaskan waters, and he became their youngest partner. The company proved so successful that it paid the United States Government considerably more in rights than the total cost of the Alaskan purchase.

The Captain was now ready for a less rigorous mode of life and as Mrs. Niebaum did not share his love for the sea he turned his thoughts to the land and to an enterprise that both could enjoy.

On various trips that he had made to Europe on behalf of the Alaskan company he had become increasingly interested in viticulture and wine making. He had visited many of the European wine growing districts and had collected a large number of books on the subject. His hobby finally became his life's destiny. With enough time and money to accomplish his purpose he decided to attempt producing in California wines comparable to Europe's finest.

After a thorough search for the most suitable location Captain Niebaum purchased in 1879 a portion of the old Mexican Caymus Rancho grant, extending from Rutherford up to the slopes of Mount St. John, highest peak of the Mayacamas range. The property had already been called Inglenook (Scottish for fireside corner) by the former owner, W. C. Watson. The name appealed to Niebaum and he retained it.

Captain Niebaum devoted the following years to planning, building and planting. Further trips to the wine growing regions of Europe were made where he studied every aspect of viticulture. Cuttings of the choicest wine grape varieties were shipped home. At Inglenook he established his vineyards with the utmost care and always with due regard to the beauty of Nature. The cellars and winery were built according to the most modern specifications. Inglenook had become Captain Niebaum's ship and the vineyards his sea.

By 1890 Inglenook had become a model winery and vineyard. So particular was the Captain that he used to inspect the cellars wearing white gloves and woe to the culprit if the least speck of dirt was observed. In wine making his motto was "quality and not quantity." Inglenook's vintages soon achieved the highest reputation.

When Captain Niebaum died in 1908 Inglenook was inherited by his widow. John Daniel, the husband of Mrs. Niebaum's niece, ably directed operations for her until the advent of Prohibition. His knowledge was passed on to his son, John Daniel, Jr., who has been in charge of the winery and vineyards since Repeal, first on behalf of Mrs. Niebaum and after she passed away in 1936, on his own behalf and that of his sister, Suzanne Daniel Hawkins.

Inglenook was the first winery to label many of the better known varietals as such, pioneered such wines as White Pinot,* Red Pinot,† Charbono ‡ and claims to have been the first producer of Vin Rosé in California, launching it in 1935.

John Daniel, Jr. is as justly proud of Inglenook now as his great-uncle, Captain Niebaum, was in his day. The accent is on the production of premium varietal vintage table wines and with a few exceptions each wine is the product of the single grape whose name it bears. The policy is to give the vintage designation greater value than simple age dating and to eliminate any wine that does not live up to the highest standards.

Throughout the years Inglenook has contributed much towards the establishment of definite systems applying to the appellations of origin, the vintage dating and the varietal designations. The winery practices and favors estate bottling, meaning that the wines bottled at the estate are made solely from grapes grown on the estate's own vineyards. Daniel's philosophy is aimed at the complete "chateau type" operation. For example, in the last few years certain Cabernet Sauvignon wines that have done particularly well have been labeled not only with the vintage date but with the cask number as is the practice with very fine Rhine and Moselle wines in Germany. Such wines will carry a different *Inglenook* label and will naturally cost

---

* Chenin Blanc, see white varietal table wines chapter.
† Pinot St. Georges, see red varietal table wines chapter.
‡ *Ibid.*

more. There is no doubt that due to certain circumstances not always under human control the same wine of the same vintage will mature differently in different casks. John Daniel is optimistic about public acceptance of such especially fine and more costly California wines. This is completely in the Inglenook tradition. There has been many an *Inglenook* vintage table wine which has become a rare treasure appreciated by the gourmet and true connoisseur.

The following Napa Valley table wines are available under the *Inglenook* label, all marked with their vintage year:

RED: Cabernet Sauvignon, Pinot Noir, Red Pinot (Pinot St. Georges), Gamay and Charbono;

WHITE: Semillon (moderately sweet), Pinot Chardonnay, White Pinot (Chenin Blanc or Pineau de la Loire), Riesling (Franken Riesling or Sylvaner) and Traminer;

ROSÉ: Navalle Rosé (from Gamay grapes and named after the stream that runs through the property).

California Dry Sherry and California Ruby Port are also available under the *Inglenook* brand.

NAPA COUNTY—LOWER NAPA VALLEY
The Christian Brothers (Mont La Salle Vineyards), Napa

The Mont La Salle Vineyards and Novitiate of The Christian Brothers are located high in the hills of the southwestern part of Napa County in the so-called Napa Redwoods district, some eight miles northwest from the town of Napa.

The "Brothers of the Christian Schools" as The Christian Brothers are officially called, form a congregation of the Roman Catholic Church, dedicated to the education of young men and boys. The order was founded in 1680 at Reims, France, by Jean Baptiste de la Salle, for the purpose of educating the underprivileged. Its headquarters are in Rome. Although not priests, the Brothers lead dedicated lives, having taken the vows of poverty, chastity and obedience.

The Christian Brothers first came to the United States before the middle of the nineteenth century. At present they operate one hundred and nineteen institutes of learning in the country, such as Manhattan College in New York City, La Salle Military Academy on Long Island, St. Mel's High School in Chicago, Christian Brothers College in St. Louis, St. Mary's College at Moraga near Oakland in California.

Mont La Salle at Napa is The Christian Brothers' Novitiate for California and the Western States. Here young men are trained for the work of the congregation while a school is maintained for boys of high school age and a home for Brothers who have retired after a lifetime of service. Here also the Brothers proudly follow their wine making tradition, a heritage dating back many centuries.

In California The Christian Brothers started making wine in 1879, at first for Sacramental use only and later, with the growing demand by lay circles, for the public. The Brothers are sole owners of the wineries and use all profits for the maintenance of their Novitiate at Mont La Salle, where young men are trained to carry on the educational work of the Order, and for the operation of various schools in the San Francisco Province.

Four members of the Order, Brother John, president and general manager, Brother Gregory, vice president and business manager, Brother Timothy, the chief wine maker, and Brother Lewis, the director of quality control and research, personally supervise the operation of the wineries at Mont La Salle and at St. Helena both in Napa County and at Reedley in Fresno County.

The Brothers produce more than a half million gallons of table and Sacramental wines annually in the old stone winery built at Mont La Salle in 1903. Wines requiring long term aging are brought to the St. Helena Aging and Champagne Cellars, an old stone landmark once known as the largest stone winery in the world. After reaching their peak of maturity here in the wood they are then returned to Mont La Salle for bottling and bottle aging. The St. Helena Cellars are also the headquarters for the Brothers' champagne production. Some seventy thousand cases of sparkling wines are produced annually by the Charmat process in sixteen glistening stainless steel tanks which enable the Brothers to maintain complete scientific control. The Mt. Tivy winery is given over to the production of The Christian Brothers aperitif and dessert wines and brandy.

All the Brothers' products are marketed under *The Christian Brothers* brand with the exception of their Altar wines which bear the *Mont La Salle* label.

The regular types of generic table wines and of aperitif and dessert wines, including vermouths, are available as well as (bulk fermented) sparkling wines and of course the well known *Christian Brothers* Brandy.

Among the table wines are a number of varietals, including:

RED: Cabernet Sauvignon, Gamay and Pinot Noir;

WHITE: Sauvignon Blanc (Dry and Sweet), Semillon (Dry and Sweet), Pinot Chardonnay, White Pinot (Chenin Blanc), Johannisberg Riesling, Sylvaner and Grey Riesling. A Light Muscat is also marketed, called Chateau La Salle.

Mayacamas Vineyards, Napa

Some 2400 feet high in the Mayacamas Mountains in the Lokoya district, on top of Mt. Veeder, an extinct volcano, lies this small winery enthusiastically devoted to the finer things of life. According to local authorities Mayacamas means "Howl of the Mountain Lion" and is derived from the language of the Lokoya tribe of Indians who once inhabited the region.

Mayacamas Vineyards is a family affair operated by Jack F. M. and Mary Catherine Taylor. Jack Taylor, an Englishman and graduate of Cambridge University, was for many years with the Shell Oil Company and contributed much to its expansion as president of Shell Development Company. Mary Taylor, who comes from an editorial family, has published two books on that charming form of song called Rounds and has also written the as yet unpublished story of Mayacamas Vineyards. Among her diversified talents she is an extremely gifted cook, a true "Cordon Bleu," and has recently introduced commercially three special seasonings of her own creation that are available at the winery along with its viticultural products.

The Taylors became wine growers for the simple reason that they had always liked fine wines. They decided, in 1941, on the Mt. Veeder property because of its beautiful setting, its excellent grape growing location and because there was a winery and distillery there, dating back to 1889 and known for a time as Mount Veeder Vineyards.

The distillery, completely remodeled, is now the hospitable Taylor home. The old vineyards were all ripped out, terraced at great expense, fenced to keep out the deer who are connoisseurs of the better grapes, and replanted mostly to Chardonnay, yielding the wine in which the Taylors specialize with justified pride.

In 1958, in an effort to meet the growing demand for their wines, the Taylors formed a corporation, offering the shares directly to their customers as part of their determination to retain the "family" feeling of the enterprise. With the capital thus acquired they are working towards doubling their small capacity still keeping them however in the category of small wineries where they intend to remain.

The Mayacamas wines are not available in any retail outlet nor outside of California. They can, however, be ordered by mail or picked up on a visit to the winery. A few cases are made available each year to a handful of fine restaurants but the balance of the limited production is reserved for direct purchase by the consumers.

Among his other functions at the winery Jack Taylor is the wine maker while Mary, always full of energy, finds time to write an informative Bulletin on the Mayacamas Vineyards' activities.

The two featured brands are *Mayacamas* and *Lokoya,* the former being reserved for wines made from grapes either wholly or partly grown on the estate and produced at the winery while the latter is used for wines, specially selected on account of their high quality.

The *Mayacamas* wines are all for 100% of the variety named on the label and are unfiltered, throwing therefore a certain deposit as do the best French wines. The brand is used for the top wine of the enterprise, the Vintage Chardonnay, produced entirely from grapes grown in the home vineyards. Other wines bearing the *Mayacamas* label are the Chenin Blanc or White Pinot (the latter designation being replaced by the former) and three varietal rosés: Gamay Rosé, Cabernet Rosé and Zinfandel Rosé.

Under the *Lokoya* brand the following wines are marketed: Red and White Table wine, Zinfandel, Dry and Sweet Vermouth, Black Muscat and (bottle fermented) Pinot Champagne and Sparkling Burgundy.

Solano County
Cadenasso Wine Company, Fairfield

Here at Fairfield, Solano County, in the Suisun district is to be found the Cadenasso Winery, producer of some fine table wines, including Grignolino, Pinot Noir and Zinfandel. It is a family owned enterprise now operated by Frank Cadenasso, his wife Joan and their four children. The featured brands are *Cadenasso* and *Solano Vineyards*.

The Cadenasso Wine Company was founded in 1906 when Giovanni Cadenasso, who had immigrated from Italy shortly before, started his own vineyard and winery on the Rutherford Ranch in Green Valley, north of Cordelia. In 1916 Giovanni moved to Fairfield and planted vineyards on the site where the Solano County Hospital now stands. With Prohibition wine making came to an end and the winery was dismantled and Giovanni sold his property to the County. Wine making, however, remained in his blood. So, undaunted, he started a third vineyard in 1926, aided by his son Frank, across the road from his former location. This he did in the firm conviction that Prohibition would be repealed. He had judged rightly and when Repeal came his vineyards were prospering once more.

Giovanni Cadenasso has now passed on and so Frank is now the owner, wine maker and vineyard manager, assisted, as stated above, by his family. His uncle Giuseppe Cadenasso, Giovanni's brother, was the well known painter who taught art at Mills College.

C. *ALAMEDA—CONTRA COSTA DISTRICT*

This district, as famous in its own way as that of Napa-Solano, consists of a number of separate wine producing areas.

Celebrated throughout the country and beyond is Alameda County's Livermore Valley, home of unsurpassed California wines of the Sauterne types. Some red table wine is also produced as are sparkling wines and aperitif or dessert wines of great merit. The Livermore Valley, actually not so much a valley as a wide basin, comprises two neighboring wine growing areas, the famed vineyards centering around the town of Livermore, with their gravelly vineyards, and separated from them only by some low hills to the west, the sector around Pleasanton.

Second only in importance to the Livermore Valley is southern Alameda with its wine growing center of Mission San Jose.

Contra Costa County is best known for its table wines and especially for its Gamay. Important wine growing areas are located by Mt. Diablo, which rises so majestically to a height of nearly four thousand feet.

ALAMEDA COUNTY—THE LIVERMORE VALLEY

Concannon Vineyard, Livermore

An old firm with a famous name, strong in Roman Catholic traditions and well known for its premium wines. The main accent is on the production of white table wines as is to be expected in the heart of the Livermore Valley district. Sacramental wines form a considerable factor of the winery's business.

James Concannon, the founder, was born in the Aran Islands, County Galway, Ireland in 1847 and as a youth determined to carve out a career for himself in what he called "that shining land across the seas."

He saved up enough money for his passage and after holding various jobs in the East could afford to be married by 1874 and a year later brought his bride to San Francisco.

In the West James Concannon found full opportunity to apply his energy and resourcefulness. He pioneered the rubber stamp business on the Pacific Coast and included Mexico in his travels. In Mexico City he criticized the then prevailing sanitary conditions in no uncertain terms with the result that the famed dictator of Mexico, Porfirio Diaz, sent for him. Diaz took a liking to the forthright and energetic young man and entrusted him with full authority to remedy the situation.

The rubber printing stamp, however, was what made Concannon's fortune. By 1883 he had amassed sufficient capital to settle down with his family and farm. It was at the advice of his friend, the colorful Archbishop of San Francisco, Joseph S. Alemany, that James Concannon decided to produce wines for religious use and that he purchased, in the Livermore Valley, a suitable ranch from Horace Overacher, a homesteader. Concannon's success as a vineyardist and wine maker became rapidly established and the high traditions he set have been carried on down continuously to this day.

After James Concannon passed away in 1911 management of the winery devolved on his son, James S. Concannon, the present head of the firm. "Captain Joe" as he is known to all, is a figure of profound charm, energy and wit. A former U.S. Cavalry officer, the military touch at Concannon is nearly as evident as that of the master wine grower and the fact that he is a devout son of the Roman Catholic Church. Concannon wines are familiar to Catholic dioceses near and far, including the Vatican.

Captain Joe has managed the winery for more than forty years with the sole exception of the 1916–1918 period when he joined the cavalry to take part in General Pershing's expedition against Pancho Villa in Mexico. During Prohibition Concannon Vineyard continued to operate, producing altar wines as permitted by the dry laws.

The third generation of the Concannon family is taking over

control. Captain Joe continues as president, aided by his two sons, Joseph Jr. in sales and management and James who is the wine maker and chemist. Mrs. Concannon who is vice president of the firm and two daughters complete the picture of the family owned business.

The Concannons have effected a considerable replanting program providing them with varieties to produce their new Moselle, launched in 1956, their Riesling which entered the market in 1959 and their Champagnes which were added to the Concannon line in 1958 in commemoration of the 75th year of the firm's wine making.

Concannon Vineyard is the brand featured and the following varietal table wines are marketed, all with the Livermore Valley designation of origin on the label:

WHITE: Dry Semillon (Vintage), Sweet Semillon, Sauvignon Blanc (Vintage), Riesling (Vintage, 100% Franken Riesling or Sylvaner);

RED: Cabernet Sauvignon (Vintage).

Generic white and red table wines from the Livermore Valley are also available including the Cardinal Rosé. Chateau Concannon is sweet and made from a blend of late picked Sauvignon and Semillon grapes. The popular Moselle is one of very few table wines on the market bearing this name.

Aperitif and dessert wines are also marketed including a Vintage Muscat de Frontignan, a sweet dessert wine with a pronounced but delicate perfume and flavor.

The *Concannon* Champagnes (see also above) are bottle fermented and produced from the Concannon Livermore Vineyards. They include a *Brut,* one of California's driest with a sugar content of less than 1% and an *Extra Dry,* in the medium range of dryness.

Cresta Blanca Wine Company, Livermore

Founder of the famed Cresta Blanca winery was that California wine pioneer Charles A. Wetmore who purchased part of the old

Rancho El Valle de San Jose in Livermore in 1882, planted his vineyards with selected imported cuttings and built the winery in 1883. He named it Cresta Blanca after the limestone ridge which dominates the vineyards where a landslide exposed a great white crest, sliced off the hillside as by a giant's carving knife.

Charles Wetmore was born in Portland, Maine, in 1847 and came to California with his parents when he was nine years old. After attending public schools in Oakland he entered the newly established University of California graduating with the very first class, of which he was valedictorian. He worked as a reporter on various newspapers, including the *Alta California* and the *San Francisco Chronicle*. Deeply interested in viticulture he was appointed in 1878 as a delegate of the California State Viticultural Society to visit the Paris Exposition. During this trip he made a thorough study of French wine growing methods. On his return he organized the Board of State Viticultural Commissioners and served on it with prominence for a number of years. As an official of the California wine industry, as a wine grower and as the author of treatises and articles on viticulture and wine production Charles Wetmore was recognized as an outstanding authority on California wines for over half a century.

Wetmore considered that the gravelly soil at the mouth of the Arroyo del Valle in Livermore Valley offered every condition essential for the growing and producing of the finest wines of the Bordeaux types. At Cresta Blanca he planted vines brought over from France, among them cuttings from Château d'Yquem in Sauternes and from Château Margaux in Médoc. He was a perfectionist and the reputation of his Cresta Blanca wines soon became solidly established, their renown spreading far and wide. The "Grand Prix" awarded to Cresta Blanca at the Paris Exposition of 1889 was a reward that spoke volumes.

Clarence J. Wetmore, also a University of California graduate, became associated with his brother at an early date. In 1893 Clarence purchased the property from his brother and retained his connection with Cresta Blanca for over forty years, operating it until 1920 when he sold it to L. B. Johnson.

During Prohibition business was carried on, as allowed by the dry laws, for sacramental purposes. With Repeal the corporation was reorganized with Clarence Wetmore once more as president and Johnson as general manager. With the death of Clarence Wetmore in 1936 Johnson became the sole owner. In 1941, during the second World War, when the distilleries were suffering from a lack of spirits for their whiskies and were buying the larger wineries, Johnson sold Cresta Blanca to the Schenley interests who have since operated the enterprise.

Myron S. Nightingale who has been closely associated with some of the wine industry's most important experiments and achievements, is the resident manager at Livermore. A bonded winery is also maintained in San Joaquin Valley at Delano where Chet Steinhauer is the resident manager.

Cresta Blanca produces table wines, aperitif and dessert wines and sparkling wines of premium quality. The winery features its white table wines from the Livermore Valley and its red table wines made from grapes grown in the Napa and Sonoma Valleys. It is a leader in the field of premium sherries, using *flor* sherry in the blending process while premium quality ports and vermouths are also produced.

All wines are marketed under the *Cresta Blanca* brand. Generic table wines comprise a sweet Chateau Sauterne and a Vin Rosé while the varietals include:

WHITE: Premier Semillon,* Dry Semillon, Sweet Semillon, Sauvignon Blanc; Pinot Chardonnay; Grey Riesling;

RED: Cabernet Sauvignon, Pinot Noir, Zinfandel.

---

* A very interesting wine, launched recently after long experimentation. It is sweet, rich and fruity and made from hand picked Semillon grape clusters held, before crushing, in the environment of a culture of *Botrytis Cinerea,* the famed fungus that, under favorable conditions, forms naturally on overripe grapes in the Sauternes district of France and along the Rhine and Moselle in Germany, imparting to the resulting wines a luscious sweetness. Production of the Premier Semillon is naturally quite limited.

The *Cresta Blaca* sparkling wines are bottle fermented, featuring Champagne (medium dry, available also in Magnums, *Brut* Champagne (dry), Pink Champagne and Sparkling Burgundy.

Aperitif and Dessert wines include "Palomino Sherry" as well as the outstanding specialty Sherries named "Dry Watch" and "Triple Cream."

The winery produces a Dry and a Sweet Vermouth as well as an Extra Dry or White Triple Dry specially suited for those who favor a very pale and very dry Martini.

Wente Bros., Livermore

Bearing one of the greatest names in the California wine industry, the brothers Wente are the producers of some of the finest white table wines of the country, notably of the sauterne and white burgundy varieties.

Carl H. Wente, the founder of the firm, was a native of Hanover, Germany, and came to this country in 1880. He received his first experience in California wine making under the personal supervision of Charles Krug, the great pioneer viticulturist of Napa Valley. Carl Wente soon branched out for himself and purchased, late in the fall of 1883, some vineyards in the Livermore Valley south of the town of Livermore. On this land the original Wente winery still stands.

From the beginning Carl Wente specialized in the production of the finest quality table wines, for which he found a ready market and at prices considerably higher than the average at that time. Both the Semillon and Sauvignon blanc grapes of the Sauternes region in France soon proved themselves to be particularly well suited to the Livermore soil and climate, and so, later on, did the Pinot Chardonnay of white burgundy and champagne fame.

Gradually the Wente holdings were extended, first by the founder and later on by his sons, Ernest and Herman Wente, the present owners. An important acquisition was that of the neighboring El Mocho vineyards. When that highly regarded wine growing pioneer of the Livermore Valley, Louis Mel, retired at an advanced age, he sold his treasured El Mocho property to the Wentes. Mrs. Mel-de-Bire was a friend of the contemporary Marquis de Lur-Saluces, owner of the world renowned Château d'Yquem in Sauternes, near Bordeaux in France, and when Charles Wetmore, as delegate of the California Vinicultural Society and the founder of Cresta Blanca, was charged with obtaining cuttings of the finest European vine varieties, she gave him a letter of introduction to the proprietor of Yquem. Wetmore returned with cuttings of the Semillon, Sauvignon blanc, and Muscadelle du Bordelais vines from the vineyards of Château d'Yquem itself and naturally gave some to Louis Mel, who propagated them in his El Mocho vineyards. When the present Marquis de Lur-Saluces visits California, he never fails to call on the Wentes to enquire how his "California Yquem children" are faring and to taste with appreciation what California is capable of producing in the way of sauternes.

The Wentes have never ceased to concentrate on creating the very best. Ernest Wente is more the farmer and wine grower, while Herman specializes in the wine making and sales end of the enterprise. They are assisted by Karl L. Wente, grandson of the founder.

Much of the soil of the Wente vineyards is alluvial deposit, washed down from the hills to the east and containing considerable heavy gravel, well suited to the finer grape varieties that like to mature the hard way. The sight of these gravelly vineyards is a perpetual source of wonderment to the novice.

The grapes are picked, variety by variety, at the peak of ripeness for wine making. The juice is pressed in small batches; the wines racked in small cooperage, then aged in oaken puncheons, and finally aged again in glass to maturity.

Herman Wente, unassuming and simple in his ways, is a great wine maker and there are many who say he is the greatest in California.

The Wente brothers are optimistic as to the future and are planting more vineyards to the fine varieties so suited to the Livermore area. The winery, too, is being gradually modernized with new bottling equipment and is air-conditioned for the best protection of their wines.

The famous specialties of the Wentes are their white table wines, unsurpassed in California. They all carry the *Livermore* designation on the label and most of the varietals also carry the vintage date. *Only* table wines are produced, all marketed under the *Wente Bros.* brand with the exception of Chateau Wente which carries the original *Valle de Oro* label, the romantic name which the Spaniards gave to the Livermore Valley.

The following *Wente Bros.* wines are available:

In the Sauterne style bottle: Dry Semillon, Sweet Semillon and Sauvignon Blanc. Chateau Wente, produced from a blend of Semillon and Sauvignon blanc with the addition of a little Muscadelle du Bordelais and as fine a sweet wine of the Sauterne order as can be produced in California is only available in the Western part of the United States as the amount of the wine is limited.

In the Rhine wine style bottle: Grey Riesling.

In the Burgundy style bottle: Pinot Chardonnay, Pinot Blanc and Chablis.

Although the Wente winery is best known for its white table wines it also produces Burgundy and a very popular Vin Rosé made predominantly from the Gamay grape with a small addition of Pinot noir.*

Garatti Winery, Pleasanton

Frank Garatti, a native of the Italian province of Lombardy, founded this firm in 1902. He planted the vineyards and operated the winery until his death in 1948. His son-in-law, F. W. (Bill) Brenner took over till he, in turn, passed away in 1960.

Most of the firm's business is derived from the sale of generic and varietal table wines in bulk to other wineries, but some wines are also marketed directly under the *Garatti* brand. These include Burgundy, Sauterne and the usual aperitif or dessert wines.

* A fine Claret is also available but only directly from the winery.

Ruby Hill Vineyard Co., Pleasanton

Ruby Hill is a beautiful wine growing ranch with tall and stately palms lining the driveway to the residence, with vineyards stretching out on all sides. The great winery, which lies beyond the residence, was built in 1887 by John Crellen, later succeeded by C. L. Crellen, and by whose family name the estate was known for many years. In 1921 the property was purchased by Ernest Ferrario, the present owner and wine maker.

Ernest Ferrario was born near Lake Como in Italy and came to this country in 1901, first settling in New York and then in California. He worked on the railroads in San Raphael and in the brickyards in San Francisco. Accustomed to wine in his native country, he had always been interested in wine making, but what made him go into the wine business in California, according to his own story, was Prohibition. The reason for this had to do with the high prices obtainable for grapes grown for home wine makers, as allowed by law. During the dry period he also made wine for medicinal and sacramental purposes.

Ferrario has developed Ruby Hill into a magnificent vineyard property. He does all of his own wine making, selling most of his production to other wineries. At the same time Ruby Hill is a popular place for those who like to buy their wines at the winery itself, be it by the case or barrel.

Under the *Ruby Hill* brand the following premium table wines are available as well as Sauterne and Burgundy:

WHITE: Semillon, Malvasia Bianca, Chardonnay and Riesling.

RED: Barbera and Zinfandel.

SOUTHERN ALAMEDA COUNTY
(Mission San Jose District)

Weibel Champagne Vineyards (Weibel, Inc.), Mission San Jose

Weibel Champagne Vineyards, founded in 1939, produces champagnes, table and aperitif and dessert wines which have established an excellent reputation for themselves. They market their wines not only for the public but also supply many a winery. It is a family enterprise, owned and operated by Rudolf Emile Weibel, chairman of the board and treasurer and his son Frederick E. Weibel, president and general manager.

The Weibels are natives of Münsingen, Canton of Bern, Switzerland. Rudolf Weibel had been engaged in the wine and champagne business in his native country and in France and came to the United States as an importer of wines and brandies in 1934. He traveled all over the country and, when he came to California, observed its climate and soil, the fine wine grapes which could be grown and the quality of wines it was possible to produce. Comparing them type by type with those of Europe, he made up his mind to emigrate to the United States and devote himself in California to the production of the finest wines that could be made. Sampling of the Beaulieu Vineyard wines was an important factor towards his final decision. So he came to this country in 1936 for good, accompanied by his son Frederick, better known as Fred.

Production of high quality champagne was the main ambition of the Weibels and for that reason the enterprise was called Weibel Champagne Vineyards, a name to which they have done full justice.

The Weibels first settled in San Francisco making champagne from purchased wines while looking around for a suitable winery and vineyard property. This they found in their ranch and winery near Mission San Jose * on the Warm Springs site of the old Leland Stanford Winery. Late in September 1958 the State Historical Landmarks Advisory Committee held formal dedication ceremonies on the Weibel property, erecting a landmark inscribed "Leland Stanford Winery—Founded 1869" in the presence of some 500 officials and other guests.

The site was famous long before the coming of the Spanish Conquistadores. Indians used to frequent the warm springs to benefit

* Founded by Father Junipero Serra in 1797.

by their healing capacities. It was a dedicated area and no tribal wars were fought in the vicinity.

A Spanish land grant gave a vast territory, including the Mission, to the Higuera family in 1836 who named it "Rancho del Agua Caliente" on account of its warm springs. In 1860 Clement Colombet bought a large acreage of the Rancho upon which he built a fashionable resort, the Warm Springs Hotel, surrounded by vineyards. The Hotel flourished until it was wrecked by the earthquake of 1868.

The following year Leland Stanford, railroad builder, Governor, Senator, and founder of Stanford University, bought a square mile of land at Warm Springs. His brother, Josiah, planted some 350 acres of vines there and built a winery with a capacity of some 500,000 gallons, later adding a brandy distillery. Warm Springs did a flourishing business, large quantities of "Stanford" wine being sold. Leland Stanford deeded the property to his brother Josiah, and encouraged by the latter's success in the wine business and affirming his belief that California was the world's best wine country he embarked on his famous wine growing project at Vina, Tehama County, an enterprise which lasted well into the twentieth century. The Weibels purchased their ranch in 1945 and devoted the next few years to replanting the vineyards and modernizing the winery. They have steadily been expanding their business capturing also the Eastern markets.

Weibel is the featured brand for all products sold directly to the public.

The bottle fermented *Weibel* Champagnes include *Brut, Extra Dry, Sec,* Pink Champagne and Sparkling Burgundy. Other Sparkling Wines produced are their Sparkling Rosé, Sparkling Malvasia and Moscato Spumante (Sparkling Muscat).

Both generic and varietal table wines are available, the latter including:

WHITE: Chardonnay, Pinot Blanc, Dry Semillon and Grey Riesling;

RED: Pinot Noir, Cabernet Sauvignon and Zinfandel;

ROSÉ: Grenache Rosé.

Aperitif and dessert wines, including Dry and Sweet Vermouth, are produced and include Cocktail Flor Sherry (dry), Flor Sherry (medium), Cream Flor Sherry (sweet), Solera Port and Cream of Black Muscat.

The *Weibel* Brandy is a fairly recent addition but not so the wine called "Tangor" with a flavor of tangerines, the winery claiming to be the originator of the "Natural Flavored Wines" (see Chapter VIII). Other specialty *Weibel* aperitifs are their "Amarinda," a bitters type wine and "Mandarelle," of the natural flavored class.

WESTERN ALAMEDA COUNTY

Paul Rhodes Winery, Hayward

Paul Rhodes is a fifth generation wine maker with vineyard and wine making experience along the Rhine and Moselle in Germany, in the Sauternes and Burgundy districts of France, in Brazil and Argentina and on the Niagara Peninsula, Province of Ontario, Canada, as well as in the United States. He is convinced that if the 2000 years of European know-how in wine making is properly used, as good or even better wines can be produced in California because of the excellence of the grapes grown, notably in the northern coastal counties. He joins many in wishing that the average American family would take fine table wines into their everyday living to add to the mealtime enjoyment.

In this country Paul Rhodes was connected with the Monarch Wine Company in New York and Atlanta, Georgia, and was superintendent of Cresta Blanca in Livermore under L. B. Johnson's ownership before he founded his own winery at Hayward in 1938.

There are no vineyards around Hayward and the Paul Rhodes wines are either produced from grapes grown in other nearby areas or are selected, blended and bottled at the winery. Paul Rhodes, with his years of wine making experience, is also a gifted blender, blending and aging his wines to a high standard of quality.

Table wines are the specialty but a full line of aperitif and dessert wines, including vermouths, are also marketed, all under the *Paul Rhodes* brand. An important part of the enterprise is the retail outlet.

Contra Costa County

J. E. Digardi Winery, Martinez

Of the Contra Costa County wineries that of Joseph E. Digardi is the best known and most representative. The winery was founded in 1886 by Frank Digardi, a native of Sicily, where cousins still own vineyards in the neighborhood of Palermo. Frank Digardi planted vineyards on the slopes of Mount Diablo and later acquired and developed other vineyard properties in the county.

The enterprise is owned by Joseph E. (Joe) Digardi, son of the founder and a well known personality in the wine industry, and by his family. Joe Digardi is less active in the business than he used to be but he is ably assisted by his two sons, Francis and Ernest. Family holdings include vineyards in the Clayton Valley lying in the shadow of Mount Diablo and in the Vine Hill area south of Martinez.

Red table wines are featured with *Digardi* the brand for wines of premium quality. Most notable among these is the *Digardi* Mountain Gamay which has deservedly made quite a reputation for itself. In 1959 a new wine was added to the list, a Charbono, made from a grape said to originate in the Piedmont region of Italy.

Gopher Gulch Wine Cellars, Walnut Creek

This is an excellent example of a small private winery operated simply for the pleasure of making wines as a hobby and for that reason is treated more extensively than its size would warrant. It is permissible by federal law to operate a non-commercial winery producing not more than two hundred gallons yearly.

Owner of Gopher Gulch Wine Cellars is James Pomeroy Howe, who since giving up newspaper work has made a name for himself in his experiments in wine making.

Jim Howe was born in Atchison, Kansas, on the Missouri River, where his father, Ed Howe, ran the Atchison *Globe*. Ed Howe, known as the "Sage of Potato Hill," wrote several books, the best known being *The Story of a Country Town,* which Mark Twain liked so much he penciled a nine-page letter about it, now a treasured document of the Howe family.

Perhaps the fact that the Brenner brothers in Atchison, when Jim Howe was a youngster, made dry red wines from their Doniphan vineyards inspired the budding journalist's later hobby. Jim Howe first followed his father's footsteps and worked with newspapers all over the country, including the *Evening Journal* in New York, the *Times-Democrat* in New Orleans, the *Oregonian* in Portland, the *Bulletin* in Honolulu and the *San Francisco Chronicle*. At one time he ran the *Index* at Emmett, Idaho. He joined the Associated Press in 1914 and was a correspondent with the U.S. Forces during the First World War. He traveled extensively over the world, including Russia, and was stationed at one time or another in London, Paris, Berlin, Warsaw, Peking, Tokyo and Singapore.

Jim Howe's winery is, as he himself calls it, an experimental one. He obtains grapes from well-known wine growers, such as the Wente Bros. of Livermore, John Daniel Jr. of Inglenook, and Dr. Maynard Amerine of the University of California to see what can be accomplished with the grapes for purposes of comparison. On the whole he has had better luck with the whites than with the reds.

The resulting wines are labeled with the *House of Howe* name, with indication both of the grower who supplied the grapes and of the particular variety. Thus there is, for example, a House of Howe Pinot Chardonnay, Vintage 1952, Grapes from Wente Bros., produced and bottled by Gopher Gulch Wine Cellars.

A feature of the cellars of Gopher Gulch Ranch is the fabulous collection of vintage wines, both European and Californian. Here can be seen such vintages, all of the better years, as Romanée Conti, Château Latour, Château Cheval Blanc, Martin Ray, Beaulieu, Inglenook and others of the top-flight California class. Jim Howe has a passion too for magnums, a bottle seen and cultivated only too rarely in California. Many an expert has said with reason that a great wine achieves its ultimate greatness when bottled in the imposing and comfortable magnums.

D. *SAN FRANCISCO*

California Wine Association, San Francisco

This famous old company has a long history dating back to 1884 when a number of California's well known wineries joined to form the original California Wine Association. Membership has varied over the years but the company has always played an important part in the California wine industry. In 1929 it was reorganized as Fruit Industries, Ltd. but reverted back to its former name in 1951.

For many years A. R. Morrow was the dominant figure of the firm. The memory of this "grand old man" of California viticulture will always be cherished and his name is perpetuated in one of the company's familiar brands. N. H. Gordon is president of California Wine Association, Sydney C. Wortley is chairman of the board, W. L. Kiggens is executive vice president, W. Perelli-Minetti secretary, L. S. Durrell treasurer, Mario Perelli-Minetti is general manager, Aubrey Harwood Jr. assistant general manager and Stanley Strud production manager and director of quality control.

California Wine Association is composed of a number of cooperative and other wineries which are located in the major wine growing districts of California and to which a large number of grape growers contribute their grapes. In this manner the company can obtain the various types of wine where it is most advantageous to do so with regard to regional suitability and quality.

The main offices of the company are located in San Francisco. The Association completed a large combination warehouse and bottling plant in Lodi in 1959 while its producing plants expanded their facilities.

The member wineries are the following: Cherokee Vineyard Association at Acampo, Lodi Winery, Inc., and Rancho del Oso Winery, both at Lodi, Delano Growers Cooperative Winery and A. Perelli-Minetti & Sons, both at Delano. In addition wines are obtained on a selective basis from another dozen wineries.

California Wine Association is one of the largest producers in the state and its wines and brandies enjoy a national distribution, the brands varying somewhat according to region and locality.

Table wines and aperitif and dessert wines, including vermouths, as well as sparkling wines and brandy are produced and marketed.

Ambassador is the featured brand for the premium wines of all types while *Eleven Cellars, Greystone* and *F. I.* are other well known brands of the company. *A. R. Morrow* and *Aristocrat* are the labels restricted to brandy. "Red Rooster" is the name given to the natural flavored type wine marketed by the Association.

E. *SANTA CLARA—SANTA CRUZ AND SAN BENITO DISTRICT*

The neighboring counties of Santa Clara and Santa Cruz, with the Santa Cruz Mountains forming the border between the two, are usually grouped together as one wine growing district. Extensions of this district include the wine growing areas in San Benito County and in San Luis Obispo County.

Santa Clara County can be divided into three wine growing areas, spreading west and east from the Santa Clara Valley floor to the adjoining hills and mountains.

West of the Santa Clara Valley, in the foothills, lies Los Gatos, and higher yet, in the hills beyond, Saratoga, together forming the Los Gatos-Saratoga area. Here are the homes of some of the finest table wines and champagnes of California, while fine aperitif or dessert wines are also produced.

To the east of San Jose lies the hillside Evergreen area with its vineyards stretching onto the slopes of Mt. Hamilton. From this section hail a number of superior table wines.

The southern part of Santa Clara County and of its valley is noted for an important winery section, centering around Morgan Hill, San Martin and Gilroy, with good wines of all types being produced from the neighboring hillsides. Many a sound "country" table wine also is produced in the small wineries, run mostly by Americans of Italian descent, in the section west of Gilroy up towards the Hecker Pass and in the Uvas area.

Santa Cruz County is equally noteworthy for its wines. Some excellent table wines are produced above Felton and at Soquel. Besides there are scattered vineyard areas in the county including Vinehill, towards Los Gatos, Bonny Doon, southwest of Ben Lomond, Boulder Creek, north of that Scottish-named elevation, the Laurel area in the mountains towards the Santa Clara County line, and the Casserly section, up towards Mt. Madonna.

San Benito yields some fine table wines south of Hollister, while San Luis Obispo County, where Paderewski once grew his wine grapes and almonds, is noted for its hillside table wines, especially Zinfandel.

SANTA CLARA VALLEY—LOS GATOS, SARATOGA AREA
Almadén Vineyards, Los Gatos

About midway between Los Gatos and the former quicksilver mining village of New Almadén * and some five miles south of San Jose are to be found the winery and domain of Almadén, overlooking the undulating hills towards Loma Prieta and the Mountains that separate Santa Clara and Santa Cruz Counties. Here some of the finest California champagnes are produced as well as table and aperitif and dessert wines of great merit.

The founder of Almadén was Etienne Thée, a farmer from Bordeaux in France who is said to have been lured to California by the Gold Rush. In any case he devoted himself to less elusive and more permanent pursuits, grape growing and wine making. To

---

* So named by the Spaniards after the quicksilver mines of Almadén in the Province of Ciudad Real, New Castile, Spain.

this end he purchased from the Guadalajara pioneer José Augustin Narvaez part of the old Rancho San Juan Batista, securing for himself a fertile tract of land along the creek called Guadalupe River. Here he planted his first vines in 1852 and later built his home, that still stands today, on a high knoll with its sweeping view of the valley and of the mountains beyond.

Thée was soon joined in his enterprise by a neighbor and compatriot, Charles Lefranc, said to have been a tailor in Passy, the suburb of Paris. The vineyards were enlarged and planted to cuttings of choice vines imported from the districts of Champagne, Bordeaux, Burgundy and the Rhône Valley. Lefranc married Thée's daughter, Adèle, and eventually inherited his father-in-law's property. He prospered together with his vineyards and by the end of the eighteen seventies could boast that they contained more vines than any other in the county and, what was more important, that his wines rated with the best. The finest cooperage was imported from France around Cape Horn, some of it in use down to the present. Many were the famous guests who enjoyed Lefranc's hospitality, among whom are said to have been numbered Admiral Farragut and Generals Sherman, Halleck and Ulysses S. Grant.

The French influence and atmosphere were dominant at Almadén and this tradition was strengthened when Lefranc hired a young Burgundian to help in the office and winery. This was Paul Masson who was to make his own name great in the California wine industry and followed precedent by marrying Lefranc's daughter, Louise. Eventually Masson became associated with his father-in-law in the production and merchandising of champagnes and table wines in a jointly owned business, Lefranc-Masson. Later he established himself on his own property in the hills above Saratoga (see Paul Masson Vineyards).

Almadén (the property was given the district name of Almadén in 1941) was inherited by Charles Lefranc's son Henry and after the latter's death in 1909 was held in trust for the family until it was sold to Charles Jones. With the advent of Prohibition Almadén entered a dormant period as far as wine making is concerned.

In 1941 Louis A. Benoist, well known San Francisco business man and president of the Lawrence Warehouse Company, national field warehousing concern, purchased the property at the advice of the noted wine authority Frank Schoonmaker. Oliver J. Goulet, one of the foremost experts in the field, was engaged as wine maker and plant manager. In this capacity he has been ably assisted since 1954 by A. C. (Al) Huntsinger, another well known figure in the wine industry. Louis Benoist is president of the company while H. Peter Jurgens is the vice president and general manager as well as sales and advertising manager.

Under the direction of Oliver (Ollie) Goulet the winery and other buildings were renovated and the original vineyards were brought into shape. Additional acreage was acquired, planted to the finest varietals.

Louis Benoist revived the tradition of hospitality set by Charles Lefranc. A charming host he receives with elegance in the villa built by Etienne Thée over a century ago. Wonderful luncheons and dinners are given, preceded by the traditional aperitif, *Almadén* Champagne *Brut* and accompanied by a selection of the ranch's choice vintages. Many a celebrity as well as near and non-celebrities have enjoyed Louis Benoist's hospitality at Almadén.

The policy is to produce wines as fine as possible. Recent winery expansions include a new champagne cellar and a sherry room featuring six Soleras, making Almadén's Solera operation one of the most modern and largest in the country. A huge binning cellar for bottle aging red table wines houses inventories of Cabernet Sauvignon and Pinot Noir with the purpose of aging red wines at least two years in glass before placing them on the market.

Almadén's acreage was increased in 1955 by the purchase of the Sykes Ranch at Paicines near Hollister in San Benito County in the area of the Pinnacles where the legendary bandit Joaquin Murietta hid out during his brief and bloody career. The rolling hills on which cattle grazed have been transformed into extended mountain vineyards to assure adequate supply and reserve of choice wine variety grapes to meet the steadily increasing demand for the finer varietal wines. Here also, at Paicines, a crushing operation and a distillery, for brandy production, are located.

San Benito County, in the area around Hollister, has for long had an enviable reputation for yielding premium wines. Its best known wine enterprise, Valliant Vineyards, is now also operated by Almadén under lease. The Paicines and Valliant Vineyards, totaling more than 2000 acres, supply Almadén with Johannisberg Riesling (for which San Benito County is famous), Gewurztraminer, Pinot Blanc, Chardonnay, Semillon and Grenache Rosé as well as Cabernet Sauvignon and Pinot Noir, the two red classics.

Another important vineyard belonging to Almadén is located at Pleasanton in the celebrated Livermore Valley white table wine district and yields Chardonnay, Pinot Blanc, Sauvignon Blanc, Semillon and Grey Riesling to complete the winery's white varietal wine production.

Almadén Vineyards produces a complete selection of premium wines marketing them under the *Almadén* label.

The sparkling wines (bottle fermented) number the *Brut* already mentioned above, and quite dry, *Extra Dry* (medium) and *Demi Sec* (on the sweet side) as well as Rosé (Pink) Champagne and the inevitable Sparkling Burgundy.

Table wines include generic types such as the Mountain Reds and Whites as well of course as the varietals, the latter listing reading:

RED: Cabernet Sauvignon and Pinot Noir;

WHITE: Dry Semillon; Pinot Chardonnay and Pinot Blanc: Johannisberg Riesling, Traminer, Sylvaner and Grey Riesling;

ROSÉ: their familiar and deservedly popular Grenache Rosé.

The three *Almadén* Sherries are of the *flor* type and blended and aged according to the Solera system: Solera Cocktail (dry), Solera Golden (medium) and Solera Cream (sweet). The Solera Ruby and Tawny Ports are also blended and aged in the same manner. *Almadén* Vermouth comes in Pale Triple Dry and Sweet types. In 1952 the winery launched its "Centennial Brandy" to celebrate the 100th year of its establishment.

Novitiate of Los Gatos, Los Gatos

In the hills above Los Gatos one finds the magnificently situated Seminary of the Sacred Heart Novitiate of the Society of Jesus and its beautiful vineyards. Here young men begin their training for missionary work in the Orient, for teaching positions in schools operated by the Jesuits in California, or for parochial duties in some of the dioceses along the West Coast.

Since its founding in 1888 the Novitiate has maintained the tradition for producing fine altar wines in strict accordance with the Canon Law of the Roman Catholic Church. Once the needs for sacramental wines is met, the remainder of the production is made available to the public through commercial channels.

The Jesuit Fathers have full charge of the production of the wines while the Jesuit Brothers supervise or carry out the actual work in the vineyards and winery. The novices and junior students pick most of the grapes each fall. Many of the vines were imported from France, as were the muscats from the Montpellier region near the Mediterranean.

Father John F. Connolly, S.J. is the president of the Novitiate while Father Henri Charvet, S.J. is the vice president and vineyard manager, Father Thomas W. McKey, S.J. the secretary and sales manager, Father Ralph J. Deward, S.J. the treasurer and general manager. Brothers Lee Williams, S.J. and George Long, S.J. are the wine makers, Fathers James E. Ransford, S.J. and Thomas D. Terry, S.J. the chemists, Brother Alan G. Mills, S.J. the laboratory technician and Brother E. Silveira, S.J. the bottling superintendent.

The Novitiate's Altar Wines are only available to the clergy. They are similar or identical to the wines marketed for the public (see below) but are in each case labeled with a distinctive name, appropriate to the particular wine.

A listing of the Novitiate's Altar Wines follows:

"Manresa" (Red Burgundy), "Villa Joseph" (Sauterne), "Vin Doré" (Sweet Sauterne), "San Carlos" (Chablis), Grenache Rosé;

"Villa Maria" (medium dry Sherry), "Novitiate" (Port), "San Ignacio" (Tokay), "L'Admirable" (Angelica), "Guadalupe" (Muscat de Frontignan), "San Jose (Red Muscat).

Available to the public under the *Novitiate* brand are the following table and aperitif and dessert wines, all in the premium class:

Table wines: Burgundy, Sauterne and Chablis in the generics and Cabernet Sauvignon, Zinfandel, Pinot Blanc and Grenache Rosé in the varietals.

Dry Semillon and Sauvignon Blanc were formerly produced separately but these are now used for reasons of economy in the Dry Sauterne and Chateau Novitiate production, the latter a sweet wine of the Sauterne type.

The Novitiate is also well known throughout the country for its aperitif and dessert wines. These include Sherry, Dry *flor* Sherry, Cocktail Sherry, Port, Angelica, a wonderful Muscat Frontignan and an altogether exceptional dessert wine (used by many as an aperitif), the Black Muscat, made entirely from blended vintages of Muscat Hamburg grapes grown at the Novitiate's Guadalupe Ranch.

Paul Masson Vineyards, Saratoga

A great name in the history of the California wine industry and a national enterprise, started by that famed Frenchman from Burgundy, Paul Masson, the origin of the enterprise dating back to 1852.

Paul Masson came to work for Charles Lefranc at his winery between Los Gatos and New Almadén, eventually marrying his boss's daughter, Louise (see Almadén Vineyards). He became associated with his father-in-law, the firm being called Lefranc-Masson. After Lefranc's death it bore the name of Paul Masson alone.

In the 1880's Paul Masson established himself on a property in the Santa Cruz Mountains above Saratoga where the soil and climate were eminently suited to the growing of the finer wine grape varieties and planted his vineyards to cuttings of the choicest imported vines. The winery Paul Masson built on this mountain property was partly destroyed by the 1906 earthquake but was rebuilt by him in the following years using some of the sandstone from the old St. Joseph's Church in San Jose which had been destroyed in the same disaster. He also obtained from the ruins of the Church a 12th century Romanesque portal which had originally come from Spain.

Paul Masson made his name forever famous by producing champagnes and table wines of the highest quality. For over half a century he worked in his steeply sloping mountain vineyards and in his wine cellars establishing a great name for his wines and becoming somewhat of a legendary figure himself. For several years he was a Viticultural Commissioner for the State of California. He made frequent trips to his native France, purchasing additional vine cuttings and the latest in winery equipment. One of the firm's earliest awards for fine wines was made at the Paris exhibition of 1900. In 1936 Paul Masson retired from his vineyards and passed away four years later, a greatly respected personality and true modern pioneer of the best that can be produced in California wines.

Before he retired Paul Masson had sold his vineyards and winery to Martin Ray who operated the enterprise with skill and success, following the tradition of producing only the best in champagne and table wines. A disastrous fire occurred in 1941, wrecking the winery and causing great losses but Martin Ray, with energy and determination, rebuilt both the winery and his business. Two years later he sold the enterprise to Joseph E. Seagram's, the distillers, later establishing another domain of his own even higher up in the mountains (see Martin Ray). Seagram's operated the Masson winery and vineyards only a short while, being succeeded in 1945 by a company in which Alfred Fromm and Franz Sichel are the partners. Both the Fromm and Sichel families have been in the wine industry for a great number of years, the former for five generations and the latter for seven. Otto Meyer is now president of the firm and his knowledge both in producing and marketing fine wines continue to place the Paul Masson name in the forefront of the premium wine field. Leo A. Berti, qualified by his specialized education and by years of experience in the California wine industry, is vice president in charge of production.

Kurt G. Opper, whose family produced fine wines in Europe for five generations, brought his skills to this country in 1939 and has been the wine master at Paul Masson Vineyards for many years. Hans Hyba, the champagne master, is recognized as one of the top men in his field. He has contributed many notable improvements to the production process of bottle fermented champagne and experts of famous French champagne houses have visited him to observe his methods, which are available to any one wanting them.

In recent years the Paul Masson firm has extended its vineyard holdings through the purchase of the San Ysidro Ranch near Gilroy which was planted to varietal wines under the supervision of University of California viticultural specialists.

In 1959 the firm opened the Paul Masson Champagne Cellars in Saratoga. In view of the historic mountain vineyards the new Champagne Cellars consolidate the bottling, packaging and shipping facilities for the entire Paul Masson line, including the brandy. In a building designed to practice generations old traditions in modern surroundings visitors have the opportunity to observe all wine aging and champagne making operations and to taste the various types of wines produced by Paul Masson. An experimental "mother vineyard" adjoins the winery. The building is of eye catching modernity with a roof consisting of four huge wood arches. It contains 121,600 square feet and what with the "Champagne" fountain 67 feet high set in a 9,000 square foot reflecting pool and a reception rotunda featuring a spiral ramp to the visitors gallery it is a most impressive sight.

The new winery is located some three miles to the east of the famous old Paul Masson winery, previously the focal point for visitors. It is here that a natural bowl forms the lovely setting for summer Sunday concerts featuring many a famous artist and it is here on the terrace overlooking the Santa Clara Valley from an imposing height that many an *al fresco* meal has been enjoyed while quaffing some fine Paul Masson table wine or champagne.

Paul Masson Vineyards, in the premium bracket, produces and markets both generic and varietal table wines, sparkling wines, aperitif and dessert wines including vermouth, as well as brandies, all under the *Paul Masson* label.

The varietal table wines include:

RED: Cabernet Sauvignon, Pinot Noir, Gamay Beaujolais;

WHITE: Pinot Chardonnay, Semillon, Chateau Masson (Sweet Semillon).

There is a *Paul Masson* Vin Rosé as well as a Vin Rosé Sec (dry), the former also available in Magnums as is the Burgundy.

The regular types of aperitif and dessert wines are marketed both in fifths and in Magnums while the Rare Dry Sherry, Rare Cream Sherry and Rare Tawny Port come in heart shaped decanters. The Vermouths include both a Double Dry and a Sweet type.

Paul Masson Vineyards are especially famous for their Sparkling Wines. These include *Brut* Champagne, available also in Magnums and Jeroboams,* Red Champagne (Triple Red), marketed in the same sizes, Extra Dry Champagne, Pink Champagne and Sparkling Burgundy (Cuvée Rouge), all three available in Magnums also.

Martin Ray, Saratoga

High above Saratoga Mt. Eden rises steeply to an altitude of some two thousand feet. It is there, on the summit of the mountain, commanding a grandiose view of the whole of the Santa Clara Valley, that Martin Ray devotes his skill to the production of table wines and champagnes comparable to the finest of France.

Born into a farming family of Saratoga, Martin Ray first became a stockbroker, a profession he followed with such success that he

*Magnums hold 2 bottles while Jeroboams hold twice again as much.

was able, at a relatively early age, to start the wine making career
he dearly ambitioned. He had set his heart on Paul Masson's
winery and vineyards above his native village and in 1936 he accomplished his desire, purchasing them from that great man when
the latter retired from his life's work. Martin Ray operated the enterprise with distinction, establishing the prestige position he has
held ever since. Desirous on concentrating on the finest varietals
exclusively—a field in which he was one of the pioneers—he sold
the Paul Masson vineyards and name in 1943 (see Paul Masson
Vineyards) but retained the original historic corporation dating
back to 1852, amending its name to his own. He then purchased,
built and planted his present domain which adjoins his former
property but is situated on even loftier heights.

Martin Ray—Rusty as he is known to his friends—has become
somewhat of a legendary figure in his lifetime. He is a dynamic,
energetic and forceful personality, deeply devoted to his art and as
profoundly appreciative of truly fine wines as he is impatient with
any other. His vineyards, planted on the eastern and southern ex-
posures of the mountain slopes, are set out to three varieties only:
Pinot noir, Cabernet Sauvignon and Chardonnay. An underground
concrete pipe system with strategically located sumps ensures
proper drainage during the rainy season and preservation of the
top soil. All of the work done in the vineyards as well as in wine
making, bottling and shipping is done by Martin Ray and his immediate family or under their immediate supervision. The wines
are clarified not by filtering or fining but by racking and decanting
and therefore sometimes throw a deposit as do many of the great
European vintages.

The *Martin Ray* wines are all 100% varietal and of the best vintage years only. Any wine not measuring up to the highest standards
is disposed of and sold in bulk. The policy is to produce and market
only the finest and to improve wherever possible, regardless of
cost. Production is on a small scale, the wines being destined for
gourmets and connoisseurs and for the best restaurants and clubs.
It is not surprising that their cost is high.

Martin Ray is ably seconded in many phases of his work, as well as in his eloquent correspondence, by his charming wife, Eleanor. They are wonderful hosts, presiding over repasts that miraculously stretch out into the most unexpected hours, preceded as they are by the quaffing of vintage champagnes and enlivened by sparkling conversation and the finest of table wines.

Most fortunate also is Martin Ray in being able to select as his successor his son Dr. Peter Martin Ray, an outstanding plant physiologist who is familiar with the great European vineyards, has done considerable research on grape varieties and is an authority on wines as well as wine making.

All wines are marketed under the *Martin Ray* label and even the table wines come in champagne bottles, a house trade-mark since 1936.

The following table wines and (bottle fermented) champagnes are or will be available, the vintages in each case being listed in order of excellence, the relative ratings having been supplied by the producer:

Table Wines

Pinot Noir

1958 (to sell at a premium price) –1954 Third Crush (the grapes having been allowed to stay on the vines until they had raisined with the resulating wine bigger in alcohol, bouquet and flavor) –1955 –1954 (regular).

Cabernet Sauvignon

1952 Centennial Year (to be sold at a premium price under a special label celebrating the 100th anniversary of the firm's founding) –1947 –1948 –Mariage 1946–1949 (a blend of these two vintages).

Chardonnay

1959 Doctors' Cuvée (named in honor of Martin Ray's son and daughter-in-law, Drs. Peter and Terry Ray, Peter Ray having been in full charge of wine making that year; the wine to be marketed under a special label at a premium price) –1958 –1957 and 1956.

Pinot Noir Blanc de Noir

A rare wine made from the free run juice of the Pinot noir grape, a big, rich, completely dry still white wine with the unmistakable aroma and bouquet of the grape: 1956 –1957.

Champagnes

Madame Pinot: A *Blanc de Noir* Champagne made entirely from the free run juice of the Pinot noir grape: 1958 –1954 –1957 –1955 –1956.

Sang-de-Pinot (Blood of the Pinot): A coral pink champagne produced from the first light pressing of Pinot noir grapes: 1955 –1954 –1953.

Champagne de Chardonnay: From the Chardonnay grape and the rarest of the *Martin Ray* champagnes: 1959 –1958 –1956.

As time progresses the vintages listed above will naturally be superseded by later vintages.

Mt. Eden Vineyards, Saratoga

Mt. Eden Vineyards was purchased in 1960 from Martin Ray by some twenty-five distinguished professional men who formed a corporation for the purpose of growing the finest wines, regardless of cost. The enthusiasts, founding members of this exclusive wine growing club, include Dr. Ralph Isaac of Portland, Dr. William Barrett of San Francisco, Dr. Kenneth Mark Colby of San Francisco, Dr. Arturo Fallico, professor at San Jose State College. Members of other professions include the well known actor Burgess Meredith, long time *aficionado* of great wines.

The property consists of 160 acres of mountain land with a planting of 60 acres devoted to four of the great grape varieties: Cabernet Sauvignon and Pinot noir in the reds and Chardonnay and White Riesling in the whites. It was named after the Mt. Eden and Vineyards Company founded in 1888 by a group of Englishmen on part of this same land which gave the mountain its name. The vineyard is spectacularly located on a broad hogback of the mountain at an elevation of 1500 feet adjoining the Paul Masson Vineyards property.

The group is building an impressive chateau with a great club room for entertaining and wings providing quarters for vacationing members and guests, located on a dramatic rise at an 1800 foot elevation with a sweeping view of the vineyards below and the Santa Clara Valley beyond.

The wines will be fermented in small cooperage of Burgundian oak in the extensive cellars beneath the chateau. The first harvest of Mt. Eden Vineyards grown grapes will take place in 1963; in the meantime wine will be produced from purchased varietals including Cabernet Sauvignon and Chardonnay.

Mt. Eden Vineyards will market its wines under the *Martin Ray* label but with the words "Mt. Eden Vineyards, Prop." to distinguish them from Martin Ray's own wines which will indicate "Martin Ray, Prop."

Gemello Winery, Mountain View

This small family winery, founded in 1934 by John Gemello, is situated right off the busy El Camino Real in Mountain View and produces and markets wines, for sale mostly in its flourishing retail outlet on Highway 101. John Gemello, born near Asti in Piedmont, Italy, the home of some of Italy's most famous wines, retired in 1944 and Mario Gemello, his son, is now president of the enterprise. John Gemello, it may be noted, once worked in the vineyards of and made wine at the original Montebello winery in Cupertino. Little could he have dreamed at that time of the myriads of cars swooshing along El Camino Real in Mountain View and of the enterprise he started, hard to find for those in a hurry but still easy for those who want to locate a small and select winery and retail outlet.

The Gemello Winery specializes in the finer varietal table wines although the usual types of aperitif and dessert wines are also available, purchased and marketed under the *Gemello's* featured label, *Mountain View* being the secondary brand.

The finer varietal table wines are either purchased or produced at the winery and aged in small oak casks or puncheons and include:

RED: Cabernet Sauvignon, Pinot Noir, Gamay, Zinfandel, Barbera and an especially noteworthy Cabernet, made from 100% Cabernet Sauvignon grapes and on the average 8 years old, produced from grapes grown in the Saratoga foothills on land once owned by Paul Masson;

WHITE: Pinot Chardonnay (from grapes grown in the Black Mountain area in Santa Clara County) Pinot Blanc (from the Saratoga district), Semillon, Sylvaner, Grey Riesling and Riesling (a blend);

ROSÉ: Grenache Rosé. Gamay Rosé and Cabernet Rosé.

SANTA CLARA VALLEY—SAN JOSE, EVERGREEN DISTRICT
Mirassou Vineyards, San Jose

The type of operation at Mirassou Vineyards is a unique one, consisting of producing varietal table wines and champagne stock of premium quality to be sold in bulk to other wineries. Only a very limited quantity of these wines is bottled and sold to consumers direct either through mail orders or visits to the winery.

Mirassou Vineyards grow about 90% of the grapes used in the making of their varietal wines and have spent over one hundred years in determining which varieties grow the best and produce the finest wines in the Santa Clara Valley, world renowned for its quality fruit. While the legal minimum requirement for varietal labeling is 51% the varietal wines from Mirassou Vineyards are bottled at nearly 100% from the grapes after which the wines are named.

The enterprise is presently operated by Edmund A. and Norbert

C. Mirassou, fourth generation wine growers, who are continuing the tradition started in Santa Clara Valley by their great-grandfather Pierre Pellier in 1853. It is located in the rolling hills between the Santa Clara Valley and Mount Hamilton in the district known as Evergreen.

The following varietal table wines are available to the public under the *Mirassou* label:

WHITE: White (Johannisberg) Riesling, Riesling, Sylvaner, Pinot Blanc and Semillon (dry);

RED: Cabernet Sauvignon, Gamay Beaujolais and Zinfandel;

ROSÉ: Grenache Rosé.

Sparkling wines (bottle fermented) are also produced and bottled handsomely under the Mirassou Vineyards label. They include Champagne *Brut,* Pink Champagne and Champagne Rouge.

SANTA CLARA VALLEY—MORGAN HILL AND GILROY-HECKER PASS DISTRICT

Richert & Sons, Inc., Morgan Hill

Walter S. Richert, a 1932 graduate from the University of California, is a remarkable man and there are many who say he is brilliant. He is certainly very modest by nature. He first entered the wine industry in 1937 and has been connected with wineries in various capacities as chemist, wine maker, production manager, sales representative and general manager. He has held important positions in the American Society of Enologists (wine makers) and has been Editor of both *Wine Review* and *Wines and Vines.*

In 1953 he founded his own winery at Morgan Hill on a shoestring and has made good, expanding gradually as opportunities permit. In 1958 he took over the old Paradise Valley Winery at Oak Glenn a few miles west of Morgan Hill where he operates both the vineyard and the winery.

The Richert policy is to produce and market good wines at reasonable prices. Every year more and more of Richert's own wines are produced in addition to those he selects for their special qualities. Eventually all the table wines will be made at the winery. Walter Richert has great plans for the future including that of his children Robert, Eric, Scott and Barbara Jean who in one way or another all take active part in the family enterprise and, in spite of their youth, already have their own Social Security numbers. Last, but very far from least, is his wife Marion, well known for her gourmet cooking.

A retail outlet is maintained in the front part of the Richert home facing Highway 101 at Morgan Hill right next door to the former Madrone Winery now no longer in existence. At irregular times, all too few, he issues to his clients and friends *The Richert Report,* a witty and informal journal on what's going on at the Richerts. A unique retail outlet and tasting room is also maintained on Ocean Avenue in Carmel, managed by a wine expert of long standing, Robert B. (Bob) Read.

The primary brand used for wines of premium quality is *Richert & Sons* and when four graduated casks appear on the label, the answer is not far to seek; they represent Walter S. Richert and his three sons.

A full line of table, sparkling, aperitif and dessert wines, including winery produced vermouths, are available; also a Strawberry Wine, made at Madrone in the Santa Clara Valley, one of the great strawberry growing districts of the world.

Varietal table wines include Cabernet Sauvignon and Zinfandel in the reds; Semillon, Sylvaner and Riesling in the whites; Grenache Rosé.

Featured are the *Richert & Sons* premium Sherries and Ports: Vintage 1947 Pale Dry Sherry, Vintage 1947 Club Sherry (Light Cream) and Triple Cream, all from Palomino grapes; Vintage 1947 Tawny Port, Tinta Madeira Port and Triple Velvet Port. Later vintages will eventually supplant those currently marketed.

San Martin Vineyards Company, San Martin

In the heart of the Santa Clara Valley's vineyard land lies the well known San Martin Vineyards Company. This family enterprise is owned by the closely knit Filice family which originally came from the Province of Cosenza in Calabria, Italy and members of which are spread all over Central and Southern Europe. The Italian firm of Bozzo and Filice of Donnici's antecedents in the wine business are said to date back to around the year 1700.

A branch of the Filice family settled in California in the Santa Clara Valley in the early eighteen eighties and planted considerable land there in the early part of the century. In 1932 Bruno Filice, who also had wine interests in Italy, acquired the old San Martin Winery and Vineyards which had been founded forty years before. Since then a great many changes and improvements have been made in modernizing the winery and installing new equipment.

The family concern is owned and operated by Bruno Filice's children and in-laws. Michael J. Filice is the general manager while his brothers John M., Peter C. and Frank C. Filice are co-owners and also active in the concern. Their brother-in-law Pasquale Lico is also a co-owner and the wine maker. Michael Filice Jr. is the vineyard manager and Michael Bo the chemist.

Over a thousand acres of vineyards are under cultivation, most of which were planted by members of the family. They are situated on the sunny western hillsides of the Santa Clara Valley, many of them on the slopes of Mount Madonna, dominating the Hecker Pass, and include Glen Loma and Castlewood, planted to the choicer varietal vines.

A magnificent new tasting room and retail outlet was recently opened right on Highway 101 near the handsome ivy-covered San Martin Winery. Visitors entering the tasting room find themselves in an atmosphere of wine use rather than production. If they wish they can go to the elaborate wine bar with its carved oak oval backdrop where host bartenders, versed in the use of wine, assist in planning scientific tasting tests. Sales are not pushed but all the San Martin wines are attractively displayed should one wish to make a purchase.

A full line of table wines, sparkling wines, aperitif and dessert wines including vermouths and fruit wines are available, *San Martin* and *Castlewood* being the featured brands.

Among the premium table wines the following varietals can be obtained:

RED: Cabernet Sauvignon, Cabernet Ruby (from the Ruby Cabernet grape), Zinfandel and Pinot Noir;

WHITE: Dry Semillon, Sylvaner Riesling, Pinot Chardonnay and a fruity and fragrant Malvasia Bianca (from the grape of the same name);

ROSÉ: Grenache Rosé.

Chianti is also available as are the generic table wines, produced from mountain grown grapes.

The *San Martin* bulk fermented sparkling wines are fine in their class and include: *Brut* (very dry), *Extra Dry* (medium) and *Demi Sec* (fairly sweet) Champagne as well as Pink Champagne and Sparkling Burgundy. A specialty is the Spumante Moscato, a sparkling Muscat made by the traditional Italian method.

Castlewood is the featured brand for the specially aged aperitif and dessert wines, *San Martin* being used for the Dry and Sweet Vermouths and for the Berry Wines made from fresh berries from the Santa Clara Valley: Strawberry Fraisette, Blackberry (Boysenberry Variety) and Loganberry.

Montonico, a tawny wine, on the sweet side, produced from the vines of that name imported from Calabria and whose advent was already announced in this *Guide* some five years ago, is due to make its bow according to the best qualified source. Another specialty is Mokka Lau, a coffee flavored beverage. *San Martino* is the brand for table wines of the mellow, sweet, home made type: Vino Rosso, Vino Bianco and Vino Rosé.

Bertero Winery, Gilroy (Hecker Pass)

A small winery in the western foothills of the Santa Clara Valley in the Hecker Pass area.

Alfonso Bertero, the founder, was born in the neighborhood of

Turin in Italy and came to this country in 1911. He first worked for the Standard Oil Company and in 1919 went into the wine business, selling grapes to home wine makers and to other wineries for the production of sacramental wines. He moved to his present location in 1924, where he built the winery and his home. The property is part of the old Los Alamos grant and some of the original Spanish wooden stakes survive.

Bertero, who is getting on in years, has turned the family enterprise over to his son Angelo, who in turn is aided by his sons, Angelo Jr. and Carl.

Table wines only are produced, all from local grapes. Burgundy is available as well as Sauterne (from the French Colombard grape). Varietals include Pinot Noir, Cabernet Sauvignon and Semillon. Outstanding is the winery's Grenache Rosé, made exclusively from that grape. *Bertero* is the winery's main brand.

Bonesio Winery, Gilroy (Uvas district)

A winery well known in the surrounding counties, producing sound "country" Santa Clara table wines. It is located in the hilly Uvas district west of Gilroy near the Hecker Pass, *uvas* being Spanish for grapes and the region so named because the Spaniards, presumably, already raised or found grapes there. The property forms part of the former Solis Rancho, and the Bonesio residence, over a hundred years old, was once the headquarters of the large Solis Rancho grant.

Pietro (Peter) Bonesio, the founder of the winery, came from an Italian wine making family and was born in Cardona near Asti in Piedmont, Italy. Now in his eighties, he came to the United States in 1903 and worked in subway construction in New York City. He later farmed in Louisiana and then moved to Oakland, California, where he was engaged in the concrete business. In 1915 he reverted to the traditional family occupation, first starting a winery in the Rucker district, north of Gilroy. In 1921 Peter Bonesio bought the 600-acre Solis Rancho which has been the family home since.

Peter Bonesio is still active, but turned the business over in 1932 to his sons Louis and Victor. The business is now owned and operated by Louis Bonesio who was brought up in the enterprise since his earliest days, being taught the trade by his father.

The Bonesio specialties include Grenache Rosé, Mission Rosé, White Malvasia and Zinfandel.

The winery bottles under various labels, but the *Uvas* brand label is used for their finer wines.

SANTA CRUZ COUNTY
Bargetto's Santa Cruz Winery, Soquel

Founders of this family firm were the brothers Philip and John Bargetto, sons of Giuseppe Bargetto, wine grower and wine maker from the neighborhood of Asti in Piedmont, Italy. Giuseppe came to this country but then returned to his native land. His sons, however, both came over to stay. Philip came in 1887 and worked for some twelve years in the old Delmas Winery near San Jose. John immigrated in 1909 and first engaged in the produce and grape shipping business. In 1933 Philip and John founded the Bargetto Winery in Soquel which is now owned by John Bargetto and his two sons Lawrence and Ralph, the former being the wine maker, chemist and general manager and the latter being in charge of sales. Two daughters of Philip complete the family membership of the enterprise.

The Bargetto wines are produced from grapes purchased from vineyards scattered over Santa Cruz and Santa Clara counties. Table wines are the specialty while aperitif and dessert wines, including a Marsala and Dry and Sweet Vermouth are purchased, aged and marketed to round out the line.

Bargetto is the featured brand for premium wines. Besides the regular generic types the following varietals, all 100%, are available:

REDS: Barbera, Cabernet Sauvignon, Grignolino and Zinfandel; *
WHITES: Pinot Chardonnay,* Johannisberg Riesling * and Sylvaner; *

ROSÉ: Grenache Rosé.

The wines marked with an * are exclusively Santa Cruz Mountain wines, produced from vineyards in the famed Vine Hill area. All table wines are produced and bottled at the Bargetto Soquel winery.

Under the *Winemaster* brand standard quality wines are available, featuring Santa Cruz Mountain Rhine Wine and Santa Cruz Mountain Chianti.

Nicasio Vineyards, Soquel

This winery, a relative newcomer, owned and run by Dan and Bette Wheeler, a young couple devoted to the art of making fine wines, is located some six miles north of Soquel near Santa Cruz. After three years of home wine making the Wheelers bonded Nicasio Vineyards in 1955. They named it Nicasio, meaning in American Indian "Beautiful Hidden Valley" as it describes the property so well.

Dan started wine making in the belief that fine wines should be 100% varietal, free of sulphur dioxide and stored at an even temperature the year around. To provide a perfect nest for his wines he started, back in 1952, to dig a cave into a sandstone hill down the road a little from his home. It is gradually being enlarged and is composed of a number of rooms devoted to storage and tasting purposes with an average temperature of 58 degrees F., varying but little throughout the year.

The winery may be small but the devotion inspiring it is as great as its wines are fine. Two hilltops have been cleared to make room for a small vineyard planted to Pinot noir and Johannisberg (White) Riesling. Access to the upper vineyard is by a road that winds half a mile through a redwood forest.

A neighboring vineyard is planted to Johannisberg (White) Riesling, Sylvaner, Chardonnay and Cabernet Sauvignon grapes. The Wheeler's wines are made from these grapes and from Grenache and Pinot noir obtained from hillside vineyards near Saratoga. They also produce a Rosé made from Zinfandel and bottle fer mented Champagne, with no dosage added at all, of the French *Nature* type, very dry but without harshness, made from the White Riesling and Chardonnay grapes. Plans include to produce and market a Chardonnay table wine.

Both Dan and Bette are hard workers. For Dan, the vice president and chief engineer of an electronic tube manufacturing company, the winery is also a retirement plan but far more than just a hobby. The whole operation is a family affair, with all the work being done by Bette, Dan, assisted by their two teenagers, Bob and Lorraine, chief bottle washers among their other functions. The young twins, Bart and Jane, and Thomas, born during the 1958 vintage, complete the family picture.

The packaging of the Wheeler wines is elegant, in keeping with the contents. Besides the Champagne *Nature,* the following vintage table wines are available in small quantities from the winery and by mail order:

WHITE: Johannisberg Riesling, Sylvaner;

RED: Cabernet Sauvignon, Zinfandel;

ROSE: Grenache Rosé, Zinfandel Rosé.

The Nicasio Vineyards wine labels are distinctive and individually signed, Dan signing the red wines and Bette the whites. The winery motto "Work Is the Ruin of the Drinking Classes" forms the heading of the label. The brand reads: *Wine by Wheeler.*

Hallcrest Vineyard, Felton

Some 400 feet up the slopes of the Santa Cruz Mountains, overlooking the San Lorenzo Valley above Felton, lie the Hallcrest Vineyards and winery, devoted solely to the growing of Cabernet Sauvignon and White Riesling grapes, and to the production of these two 100% varietal table wines.

The vineyards are planted on the crest of a hill and were for that reason named Hallcrest by their owner, Chaffee E. Hall, who purchased the property in 1941. A corporation attorney by vocation, practicing in San Francisco for many years, Chaffee Hall is also an enophile, knowing and appreciating truly fine wines, having developed his taste during his numerous trips to the wine lands of Europe. It is at Hallcrest that he fulfills one of the great ambitions of his life, that of producing, with knowledge and lavish care, Santa Cruz County table wines which compare in elegance, bouquet and taste with the very finest of California.

Chaffee Hall is his own wine maker and all operations in vineyards and winery are either accomplished personally or supervised by his son-in-law and manager, Penry Griffiths. The utmost care is taken, both of the vines and of all stages of wine production. The first vintages were of 1946 and these, as well as the succeeding ones, have been remarkably successful.

Cabernet Sauvignon and White Riesling are marketed under the *Hallcrest* brand, with indication of the vintage year and with the Santa Cruz Mountain appellation of origin.

SAN LUIS OBISPO COUNTY

York Winery, Templeton

Representative of good wine making in San Luis Obispo County is the York Winery, owned and operated by Wilfrid S. York and located just below the peak of York Mountain on the eastern slopes of the Santa Lucia Mountains overlooking Templeton and the valley below.

The ranch property was acquired in 1882 by Wilfrid's grandfather, Andrew York. Born in Indiana Andrew came out West from Missouri in the eighteen fifties and settled in San Luis Obispo County after first having spent some time in the Napa Valley. A proud family possession is the original deed to the land, dated 1875, made out to Jacob B. Grandstaff from whom Andrew bought it, and signed by U. S. Grant, President of the United States.

Andrew York found that the grape vines he had planted to supplement his apple orchard yielded more grapes than he could market and so, with the help of his sons, Walter, Thomas and Silas, built a small winery to take care of the surplus. Shortly after the turn of the century additional land was purchased and a large vine-yard planted of Zinfandels, selected because they mature early and thereby usually miss the early winter frosts. About that time too the winery was enlarged with the use of bricks molded and burned on the place in the ancient tradition of the Babylonians.

The York place is a historic one, as time goes, and many tales are told of how the lumber to build the original houses and winery was carted over the rough and steep mountain roads all the way from Cayucos on Estero Bay which at that time was a small flour-ishing harbor before the railroad came to Templeton. Indians used trails running through the property and camped overnight on the mountain on their way to the hot sulphur and mud baths in what is now Paso Robles, twelve miles distant. Nearby also is the San Ygnacio Ranch, established by Ignace Jan Paderewski, the great Polish patriot and world famous pianist, who raised wine grapes and had them crushed at the York Winery.

After the death of Andrew in 1913 his sons Walter and Silas took over the family enterprise which became the York Brothers Winery. Upon their retirement in 1944 the third generation wine makers, Wilfrid and Howard, continued the operation until 1954 from which time Wilfrid (or Bill as he is called) has run it in sole proprietorship.

Only one wine is produced, a fruity, zesty Zinfandel. It is made in small quantities and is available in barrels for family use as well as being bottled under the brand by which the general area is known, *York Mountain.*

XII

THE GREAT INLAND VALLEY REGION

*T*HIS VAST VALLEY region sweeps down in a fairly narrow band parallel to the coast line, from which it is separated by the mountains of the Coast Range. Some three hundred miles long, it stretches from north of the city of Sacramento down south beyond Bakersfield in Kern County. Its climate, moderately warm in the northern areas, becomes progressively hotter the farther south one comes.

The region takes in the territory of both the Sacramento and the San Joaquin river valleys. It is the home of the great California aperitif and dessert wine production, for which the climate and soil are especially well suited. Most of the vines are cultivated by irrigation.

From north to south we have the *Lodi-Sacramento,* the *Escalon-Modesto,* and the *Fresno-San Joaquin Valley* districts.

A. *LODI—SACRAMENTO DISTRICT*

This district takes in the wine producing areas of Sacramento County and of the northern part of San Joaquin County.

In Sacramento County there is a wine growing area which stretches east of the city of Sacramento down southward, where both table and dessert wines are produced. Elk Grove is a center famous for its production of berry and fruit wines.

Northern San Joaquin County contains the famed wine growing district of Lodi, which spreads out to a surrounding region some ten miles deep. Lodi is on the Mokelumne River, which flows into the San Joaquin and is sometimes referred to as lying in the upper reaches of the San Joaquin Valley. It can also be said to be situated at the juncture of the Sacramento and San Joaquin valleys and in what is known as the Central Valley.

Lodi, recognized as a separate viticultural district, is especially noted for its aperitif and dessert wines. It is the center of a vast Flame Tokay vineyard district, spectacular in the fall due to the brilliant coloring of the grapes. The Flame Tokays are mainly used as table grapes, but are also employed in many of the dessert wines produced by the Lodi wineries including the wine called tokay.

SACRAMENTO—ELK GROVE DISTRICT

Gibson Wine Company, Elk Grove

Robert H. Gibson, founder of the company, turned to the production of wines after first having been a successful stockbroker both in his home town of Cincinnati, Ohio, and in New York City.

He felt that many people would enjoy wines made from other fruit than grapes and experimented for some years in the production of berry and fruit wines. His faith was fully justified and he succeeded in developing a large market for his products. Berry and fruit wines have come into their own (see Chapter IX) and the Gibson Wine Company has become one of the largest producers in this field.

Robert Gibson, Bob as he was known to his friends, spent much of his time in Roseville, California, where he had a large cattle ranch and raised rare pheasants as a hobby. It is not surprising therefore that the trade-mark of the corporation is the *Golden Pheasant* which appears on many of its labels and is blown into most of its bottles. Bob Gibson died in 1960.

A large and modern bottling plant is maintained in Covington, Kentucky, just across the Ohio River from Cincinnati, to which the company ships its wine in bulk from California to be bottled and marketed in the Middle West and the East. A distributing and storage plant is maintained in Cincinnati.

The Elk Grove Gibson Winery, where most of the company's berry and fruit wines, as well as the table and aperitif and dessert wines are produced, was originally a gas engine works. In 1934 it was converted into a winery, Robert Gibson acquiring the property in 1943. From a small plant it grew into a modern and up to date winery, producing the best known berry and fruit wines in California.

Several years ago the company purchased the Peralta Winery in Fresno with a capacity of over 1,750,000 gallons. This plant is used for storage and for the finishing of wines.

Louis W. Schulze is now the firm's president and treasurer while Marvin B. Jones is vice president in charge of the Elk Grove and Fresno wineries.

The *Gibson* brand is used for the berry and fruit wines which include (all containing 12% alcohol by volume): Old Briar Blackberry, Old Fashioned Hard Cider, Strawberry, Boysenberry, Cherry, Elderberry, Loganberry, Raspberry, Red Currant and Concord (Grape). Blackberry and Apple are also produced at 20% strength.

Gibson's Golden Pheasant "Private Stock" and *Gibson's Pheasant* are the featured brands for the usual table and aperitif and dessert wines. *Yellow Label* is used for the Champagnes and *Red Label* for the Sparkling Burgundy.

Lodi District
(Northern San Joaquin County)
Acampo Winery and Distilleries, Acampo

The winery is named after the town of that name, just north of Lodi. Dino Barengo, a graduate of the University of Nevada, is the owner, general manager and wine maker.

Barengo has been associated with the Acampo Winery since the early forties, when it was a stock corporation of which Cesare Mondavi, who later took over the Charles Krug Winery, was president. In 1943 the Acampo Winery was acquired by the Gibson Wine Company, now of Elk Grove, and Dino Barengo managed it for that concern. Barengo then leased the winery and finally purchased it in 1946, when he became the sole proprietor.

Both table and aperitif or dessert wines of sound standard quality are produced, with *Barengo* and *Barengo Reserve* the featured brands with *Royal Stag* for Northern Nevada, where Dino Barengo has retained many connections.

The most popular of the Barengo *aperitif* or *dessert wines* are his Port (mostly from the Zinfandel grape), Sherry (from Palomino and Mission), Muscatel (from the Muscat of Alexandria), and Tokay (mainly from the Flame Tokay).

Acampo Winery and Distilleries is also the home of Joseph Dudenhoefer Co., Inc. of which Barengo is president. Dudenhoefer produces May Wine (see Chapter III) and distribution covers most of the United States including Hawaii.

East-Side Winery, Lodi

This well known winery, one of the largest in the district, is a farmers' co-operative, founded in 1934. Its name was adopted because the area East of Lodi where the winery is located is known for its particularly rich soil yielding high quality grapes.

The co-operative is formed by some hundred growing farmer-stockholders to whom all returns are made after costs and taxes have been paid. A. D. Mettler is president of the co-op, Ed Preszler vice president and K. T. Anderson general manager.

The regular types of generic table and of aperitif and dessert wines are produced with *Royal Host* the featured brand. Brandy, under the same label, is an important specialty.

Guild Wine Company, Lodi

Formerly known as the "Wine Growers Guild" the name was changed in 1959 to "Guild Wine Company" as this better describes the enterprise and its activities. It is a federation of separate co-operative wineries composed in turn of numerous individual growers. The member wineries crush the grapes belonging to their members and produce the wines while all bottling and merchandising activities are located at the central blending and bottling plant at Lodi. The company returns to its member wineries the gross proceeds of the sales less costs while the member wineries return to the growers what they received less their own costs. Both the Guild Wine Company and its producing units are strictly non-profit co-operatives.

The following are the member wineries of the company: Bear Creek Vineyard Association at Lodi, Del Rio Winery at Woodbridge near Lodi and Mendocino Grape Growers, Inc. of Ukiah, Mendocino County. This enables the Guild Wine Company to market table wines from the northern coastal region and the aperitif and dessert types from the valley vineyards of San Joaquin County.

The famed L. K. Marshall, one of the all time great figures of the California wine industry, was president of the organization from its inception until his retirement in May 1957 and passed away soon afterwards. A. J. Handel is now the president while J. C. Skinner is vice president and Harold Housh both vice president and general manager.

The regular types of table wines and of aperitif and dessert wines including vermouth are marketed under the *Guild* brand, the table wine for which the company is best known being the familiar "Vino da Tavola," a sweet red table wine of the Vino Rosso order, launched by the company as a new type of wine back in 1950. It is said to be the largest selling wine of its kind. Another popular product is the *Guild* "Bouquet Rosé."

The Lodi district has been recognized as a separate viticultural district and accordingly Guild Wine Company are marketing a

Lodi Tawny Port and a Lodi Cream Sherry under their *Guild* label. These are both distinctive wines and the appearance of the appellation of origin in the name seems a most welcome development. In this author's opinion the San Joaquin Valley's famed wine districts should receive infinitely greater recognition on the labeling than heretofore. The public and the trade should be made familiar with the fact that the San Joaquin Valley is—or should be—to the premium aperitif and dessert wines what the northern coastal counties are to the premium table wines and champagnes.

The Guild Wine Company also produces and markets Pale Dry Sherry, Cream Sherry and Tawny Port under the *Ceremony* "Old San Francisco Brand" label. These are choice Lodi district wines aged in small oak cooperage and of outstanding quality.

Ceremony is also the brand used for the (bulk fermented) Sparkling Wines (Champagne, Pink Champagne and Sparkling Burgundy) but the most celebrated products marketed under the *Ceremony* label are undoubtedly the company's straight dry Brandies, 5 and 8 years old, the latter being considered by many an expert to be the finest and smoothest brandy produced in California. The *Guild* "Blue Ribbon" Brandy is a blended and sweetened product similar in character to the majority of California brandies marketed. It should be noted that all the Guild Wine Company's brandies are produced from the Tokay grape for which the Lodi district is famous and which lends itself well for brandy distillation.

B. *ESCALON—MODESTO DISTRICT*

This district covers the wine growing areas and wineries of the southern part of San Joaquin County, from Stockton south and southeast to Manteca and Escalon; it takes in Stanislaus County from Salida on down to Modesto and also includes the Livingston area in northern Merced County.

The Escalon-Modesto district, located in the northern San Joaquin

Valley, is best known for its dessert wines, but table and sparkling wines are also produced. Some of the California wineries with the largest distribution are located in this district.

ESCALON DISTRICT
(Southern San Joaquin County)

Franzia Brothers Winery, Ripon

This family concern, located about halfway between the towns of Manteca and Escalon in the southernmost part of San Joaquin County, is owned and operated by the five Franzia brothers. They are the sons of the late Giuseppe Franzia (Joe Sr.), a native of Genoa, Italy, who immigrated to this country, settling first in San Francisco and then moving to Stockton. He purchased the Franzia ranch in Ripon in 1906 and was for many years prominent in the grape-shipping business and from 1933 until his death in 1952 in the wine producing field.

Giuseppe Franzia's sons carry on the family wine making tradition, Joseph, the youngest son, better known as Joe Jr., being the president of the firm, John the secretary and treasurer, and Frank, Louis and Salvador vice presidents in charge of the various departments. Fernando Quaccia is the wine maker and chemist.

The Franzia policy is to produce and market sound standard quality wines at popular prices. The dessert wines are all produced exclusively from San Joaquin Valley grapes and so are the white table wines. The red table wines are blends of San Joaquin Valley and north coast counties wines, the latter mostly from the Napa Valley. The main brand is *Franzia Special Reserve,* while sparkling wines are marketed under the *Franzia* label.

Petri Wineries, Escalon

Petri Wineries at Escalon in southern San Joaquin County and Mission Bell Wineries at Madera, Madera County, are the operation and production names of Allied Grape Growers, a co-operative winery association composed of some twelve hundred members, owners of medium sized or small wine grape vineyards in California. It was to this organization that Louis Petri, the youthful president of Petri of California, sold the Petri and Mission Bell Wineries in 1951, retaining the exclusive marketing rights for the whole of the cooperative's output. Two north coast counties wineries are owned for the production of dry table wines, the Forestville Wineries at Forestville and the Northern Sonoma Wineries at Geyserville, both in Sonoma County.

The organization of Allied Grape Growers was created to permit both the grower and winery to share in the profits and risks of wine growing and wine marketing. The arrangement made available to the growers a nationally advertised brand of wine in which millions of dollars were invested in advertising and sales promotion. With Allied Grape Growers producing the wines and Petri Wine Company selling them, the growers dispose of a complete sales organization headed by a family of experts and, in acquiring the wineries themselves, the growers have come in as partners.

The Petri story is one of enterprise and success, the result of hard work coupled with the necessary flair for accomplishment. Founder of the family enterprise in California was Raphaelo Petri, a native of Tuscany, Italy, who came to San Francisco in the early eighteen eighties, bringing with him the family tradition for hospitality, good food and wine. He first entered the hotel business. His Toscano Hotel on Broadway and later his Cosmopolitan Hotel on Green Street became popular meeting places where good meals and wines could be obtained at reasonable prices. Raphaelo Petri also started a wine enterprise, buying a small winery in the San Joaquin Valley and founding the Petri Wine Company in 1886. He shipped wine to numerous members of the Italian American colony in California and elsewhere, including New York City. Gradually his wine business expanded until it claimed the major share of his business attention. In 1916 he purchased a large vineyard in Escalon, San Joaquin County, near the site of the principal Petri Winery at Alba Station.

With the advent of Prohibition Raphaelo Petri retired from the wine business and his son, Angelo, concentrated his energies on the Petri Cigar Company, founded by Raphaelo's brother, Amadeo Petri. During Prohibition the Petris had another interest, the manufacturing of Italian style boots in Tennessee.

Repeal saw the return of the Petris to the wine industry. Vineyards and wineries were acquired in various parts of California and wine stocks were built up. The third generation of the family now entered the wine picture. Louis Petri, born in San Francisco in 1913, the son of Angelo, had planned to become a doctor. He had studied chemistry and physics at Stanford and at the University of California and Repeal found him a medical student at St. Louis University. He decided to use his chemistry training in the family tradition of wine making and joined his father and grandfather in rebuilding the Petri wine enterprise. He started at the bottom, rolling barrels in the firm's San Francisco warehouse but soon rose "from dirt to decanter." In 1945, at the age of thirty-two, he was president of the company.

In 1953 Louis Petri purchased Italian Swiss Colony at Asti, Sonoma County (see Italian Swiss Colony) in a spectacular deal and in 1959, in an even more spectacular one, sold all of his interests to Allied Grape Growers which he had organized in the first place. Louis Petri remains, however, as president of United Vintners, the marketing organization for Allied Grape Growers.

Robert C. McInturf is president of Allied Grape Growers while Tilden E. Gonzoli and Walter Vincent are first and second vice presidents respectively, Clarence D. Holland is treasurer, Buddy T. Iwata is secretary and Paul H. Huber general manager.

A full line of sound standard quality table, aperitif and dessert wines including vermouths are marketed as well as (bulk fermented) sparkling wines, fruit wines and brandies, all under the various *Petri* brands and labels.

The *Petri* "Crystal" brand is used for the regular types of both table wines and aperitif and dessert wines. Other products available under the *Petri* brand include the always popular Grenache

Vin Rosé, the Red Rosé and White Rosé "Party Wines," Blackberry and Loganberry Wines, Dry (French type) and Sweet (Italian type) Vermouth and the sparkling wines: Champagne, Pink Champagne and Sparkling Burgundy.

Marca Petri is used for Vino Rosso Pastoso, a mellow red table wine of the Vino Rosso order and *Viva Vino di Petri* for a light and mellow California red table wine.

Petri is the labeling used for Brandy and for the Grappa Brandy, a pomace brandy, white in color, and one of the very few produced in the State, if not the only one commercially available.

Petri's "Golden Spur" and "Silver Spur" are wines of the flavored type which have recently captured their own market.

Modesto District

(Stanislaus County)

E. & J. Gallo Winery, Modesto

The *Gallo* wines are familiar to a great many people and the success of this enterprise has been tremendous, good reasons to delve into the philosophy of the two brothers, Ernest and Julio Gallo, the owners. What is their thinking? What makes them tick? With the cooperation of the Gallo Brothers themselves, the reader will find out.

Now it is a fact that wine consumption in the United States is pitifully small (about 8/10 of a gallon per capita yearly) as compared particularly with France (43 gallons), Italy (34 gallons) or Spain (28 gallons).

Along with many others the Gallos studied this matter for years, trying to learn why Americans drink so little wine in comparison with some of those other countries, all the more surprising as the United States ranks among the larger wine growing countries of the world.

Ernest Gallo came to the conclusion that there are at least three reasons why consumption is so much greater in the foreign countries mentioned:

1. The wines of those countries are made more to the liking of their peoples than are American wines made to the American taste;

2. Wines in foreign countries are priced to encourage their widespread use in volume;

3. Wine is displayed to suggest frequent use in volume.

Guided by these basic reasons the full resources of the Gallo research organization at the winery were—and are—devoted to the development of wines that will mean to Americans what Spanish wine means to the Spaniards, Italian wine means to the Italians and French wine means to the French. The idea being to develop a wine that was necessarily different from anything produced heretofore in this country or for that matter in any country, a wine tailored to the taste of millions of Americans who would buy wine in volume if they found one to their liking. A wine, also, that would be at a price level encouraging its use as an everyday refreshment beverage as well as being served with meals.

The Gallo Winery believes it has developed such a wine, a wine that has received the typically American name of "Ripple."

We are ahead of our story. . . .

It is certain that the Gallo brothers remain dedicated to their objective, undertaken when they founded their winery in 1933, to provide American homes with good, sound wines at popular prices. They attribute their progress towards that goal to the company's continuous scientific research for new, modern ways to improve the efficiency of grape growing and of wine making and to enhance the taste appeal of wines for American consumers.

One of the keys to Gallo's growth is the company's view that because wines are perishable, the only way to establish wine as a staple beverage in the American diet is to make certain (or as certain as humanly possible) that the consumer will be fully satisfied with every bottle purchased. This is why Gallo wines are bottled only at the winery where they are made and sealed under supervision of the Company's own expert enologists in Gallo's exclusive "Flavor-Guard" bottles.

This bottle is the reason why the Gallo family in 1958, at a cost of more than six million dollars, built their own glass factory adjoining the Gallo Winery at Modesto. The glass, it is stated, protects the wine from the effects of ultra violet light rays. Gallo, it is believed, is the only winery in the world to manufacture its own bottles.

Gallo's research begins with the grapes. In the Gallo vineyards in Stanislaus and Merced Counties a large number of grape varieties are grown which the company constantly tests for its blends of wine while Gallo's viticulturists also guide other growers in producing grapes for the company.

Gallo's wines are made from grapes grown in the viticultural districts where they thrive best. In addition to the original Gallo winery at Modesto there are Gallo Cellars at Fresno and Cucamonga and eight grower owned wineries in other districts producing wine for the company under the latter's supervision.

Convinced by many years of research that glass lined steel tanks are preferable, Gallo has adopted that method of cooperage, using what are virtually giant bottles.

Modesto, the home of Gallo wines, is in the heart of the historic County of Stanislaus with its wine growing tradition dating back to about 1854 when George H. Krause, a native of Germany, laid out what was to become his famed Red Mountain Vineyard on part of the old Mexican grant El Rancheria del Rio Stanislaus.

It was in Modesto in 1933, the last year of Prohibition, that the Gallo brothers visualized the coming rebirth of the California wine industry, dormant during the dry years. They thought of creating a modern winery and planned that some day homes throughout the nation would proudly serve wines from shiny bottles bearing their name.

It was an ambitious plan for the brothers. Ernest was twenty-four and Julio a year younger. They had been brought up in the tradition of good wine, born as they were in the third generation of a wine growing family whose forebears had cultivated vineyards and made wine in Italy's famed Province of Piedmont. The Gallo brothers had been educated in the public schools of Modesto and knew about viticulture firsthand, having worked in the family's vineyards. They borrowed and scraped together enough dollars to rent a warehouse in Modesto to house a few casks and a grape crusher to serve as a winery until they could build one of their own. In that old warehouse the first Gallo vintage was crushed and fermented that same year, 1933, a historic one in the Gallo story.

A few months later they built a small wine cellar on the outskirts of Modesto. This first concrete structure on the banks of Dry Creek was carefully planned as the first unit of the winery the Gallo brothers envisioned. It was built and ready for use in 1935.

At first the Gallos made only red table wines, selling them in bulk to wholesale bottlers. In 1937 they were able to build an extension to their cellar and to install further equipment. They began to produce port, sherry and muscatel in addition to their table wines. They studied modern developments in viticulture and wine making and searched for the best types of cooperage and other winery equipment. Julio Gallo devoted himself increasingly to the development of the most suitable grape varieties in the family's vineyards and to the production of wines while Ernest Gallo studied consumer and trade problems and marketing.

In the Gallo vineyards at Modesto, which the family had owned since 1925, new varieties were grafted onto old rootstocks. Additional vines were planted to grow the choicer varieties suited to local and climatic conditions. Gradually the Gallos increased their vineyard acreage, planting vines in the Keyes district of Stanislaus County and acquiring a vineyard near Livingston in Merced County.

The Gallo brothers realized that Fresno and the Southern San Joaquin Valley region yielded grape varieties most desirable for the sweeter dessert wines while Napa and Sonoma in the Northern Coastal Counties provided the best grapes for dry table wines. Accordingly they selected grapes from these districts to complete their assortment of wines.

It was not until 1940 that the Gallos felt they were producing wines of the quality they wanted to market in bottles bearing the family label. In was in that year, another milestone in the Gallo saga, when their wines first appeared on the market. A following of consumers soon developed and Gallo advertising began.

From a small beginning in California and Louisiana the *Gallo* wines gained a steady and increasing acceptance. The company concentrated on trying to please the consumer. The Gallo brothers and their staff interviewed buyers of their wines to learn the exact characteristics of wine flavor, of dryness or sweetness and of color that would please householders. They talked to retailers and salesmen to learn what their customers wanted and they strove to get their wines efficiently displayed and stocked. Year after year they were introduced in additional markets from coast to coast and their sales continued to grow.

There is no doubt that the Gallos have contributed and are contributing much to making wine ever more popular as a national beverage in the United States.

By 1960 Gallo was marketing nearly forty types of wine, all bottled at their Modesto winery. Over thirty were of the traditional types, led by the most popular generic table wines, the usual types of aperitif and dessert wine including vermouths and two berry wines: Apple Wine and Concord Grape. In addition there are Grenache Rosé and "Paisano" the popular wine of the Vino Rosso order.

In 1957 Gallo launched its flavored aperitif wine "Thunderbird" which rapidly became very popular, to be followed the following year by "Eden Roc," golden in color and with a different taste and in 1959 by "Gypsy Rose," a pink aperitif, different again.

Here we see clearly the Gallo philosophy at work, that of introducing altogether new wines, specifically suited, it is hoped, to the American taste and thereby capturing a large market of their own. So far, they have been remarkably successful and there can be no doubt that the Gallos are smart merchandisers.

Here we are back to the beginning of our story and the "Ripple" Wines, both Red and White, launched by Gallo in 1960. They are quite special and pleasing in their way, with an ever so slight effervescence placing them in the "Table Wines Plus" class (see Chapter V).

No doubt more new wines will be produced and launched by the energetic Gallos seeking to please the American palate. One great advantage of having successful proprietary names is to have consumers guided back to one's products, the aim being not only to produce new wines but also to create a captive market.

What is the author's reaction to all of this? It is quite simple. He believes that there will always be a market for the traditional types of wine, for which California has become famous, notably for the varietals. He believes that there is also room for new types of wine, such as Gallo and other wineries have launched. If they are successful, all the more power to the launchers and to those who created them. After all, Dubonnet did not always exist in France, and neither did a number of other French aperitifs. There is nothing wrong with them and neither is there with "Thunderbird" or "Eden Roc" or "Gypsy Rose" if people like them. And as far as slogans are concerned is there any difference, in principle, between "Du Beau, Du Bon, Dubonnet" and "Everyone Goes for Gypsy Rose"?

So let us welcome all and sundry newcomers in the wine field. Only time will tell whether or not they will occupy a permanent place in the American home.

C. FRESNO—SAN JOAQUIN VALLEY DISTRICT

This great district coincides with the lower San Joaquin Valley. It is famous especially for yielding wines of the sweeter dessert types, some of which have achieved great excellence. Table wines and bulk fermented sparkling wines are also produced.

The district takes in the following counties, from north to south:

Madera, with the city of Madera the main sector;

Fresno, with its many famed wineries located in the city of Fresno and in the surrounding towns, with other famous wineries to be found in Sanger, Reedley, Parlier, Fowler, Selma and Kingsburg;

Kings, with its Hanford area;

Tulare, with the main winery centers in Dinuba, Cutler, Tulare, Lindsay, and on the Kern County line right across from Delano; Kern, with Delano and the sector east of Bakersfield down to Arvin the wine production areas.

A number of well known wineries located in this district do not produce wines directly for the public under their own brands and are, for that reason only, not discussed in this *Guide*.

MADERA COUNTY

Ficklin Vineyards, Madera

A small and unique operation, the only California winery to produce no other wines than port and the first winery in the United States that made port wines produced entirely from choice Portuguese grape varieties commercially available. The Ficklin Ports rate as the finest produced in California, being unsurpassed in quality and character with a full richness of flavor.

The Ficklin wine concern, founded in the middle of the nineteen forties, has made quite a name for itself and deservedly so. It is a family enterprise, the principal owners and operators being David (Dave) B. Ficklin, the wine maker and a well known wine judge, and his brother Walter C. Ficklin Jr., the vineyardist. Their father, Walter C. Ficklin Sr., a charming gentleman familiar with all the better things of life, has an interest in the winery and vineyards.

The senior Ficklin first came to California as a young man in 1911, making his home in Fresno County and planting his first vineyards and orchards in 1912. For many years he farmed grape and fruit ranches. In the early forties the family became interested in the idea of producing red dessert wines of top quality. They closely studied the Portuguese wine grape varieties which were being tested by the University of California under local growing conditions. The decision to establish a completely specialized vineyard complex and winery was the next step. Four of the finest Portuguese varieties were selected, Tinta Cão, Tinta Madeira, Alvarelhão and Touriga, and the vineyards planted to them exclusively. A small but modern adobe winery was built by hand and 1948 saw the first vintage harvested.

The greatest care is taken to produce the very best wines possible. The vineyards are meticulously tended to yield a limited crop of the choicest grapes. At harvest time the grape clusters are individually cut with small hand shears and all imperfect fruit is left on the vines. The grapes are left in the vineyards in wooden boxes to cool off overnight and brought to the crusher the first thing the next morning. They are first lightly crushed in stainless steel crushers, breaking the skins and separating them from the stems. The crushed grapes are transferred to small open vats where pure yeast culture is added. As soon as fermentation starts a wooden hand plunger is used to submerge and mix the skins with the juice, extracting thereby the full color and flavor of the grapes. The free-run juice is drawn off and the skins are given a further light pressing in a basket-type press, the resulting juice being added to the free-run for further flavor. At the proper stage of fermentation the juice is transformed into port wine by the addition of pure grape brandy. The wine is clarified naturally by gradual settling and racking in small oak puncheons or barrels. It is aged in oak for three years or longer and at least a further year in the bottle. Owing to this process, the Ficklin Ports, like those from Portugal, will throw a slight sediment, a sign of maturing and of age. The wines, therefore, should be poured carefully, so as not to disturb the deposit, or be decanted before serving. If disturbed, the bottle should be placed upright until the wine has had a chance to settle.

The main variety of Port available is the Tinta Port, a blend of the four varieties grown. It is a full Ruby and is marketed under the *Ficklin Vineyards* brand.

A new feature of the Ficklin operation is the use of a special pot still brandy for the spirits addition. The same grape varieties used in making the wine are employed in distilling the brandy. This gives the finished product considerable additional character, the wines possessing a harmonious bouquet and flavor when mature.

In addition a new program of Special Bottlings has been launched of Vintage Ports, available only in small quantities direct from the winery. Several vintages of Tinta Madeira have been earmarked for this special program, good news for the numerous Ficklin *aficionados*.

Initiating this program was the "Special Bottling No 1 1951 vintage, bottled in 1954, for dry palates" as the special label reads. The wines are estate bottled, the labels numbered and signed by the wine maker. An extra long 2 inch cork is used to protect the wine as is a sealing specially compounded for the purpose. The wine itself originated from a single lot selected shortly after the 1951 vintage, was aged in three choice puncheons and bottled directly from those puncheons.

FRESNO DISTRICT
(Fresno County)

Alta Vineyards Company, Fresno

This corporation, also doing business as **Cameo Vineyards Company,** is the successor to many a famous name in California's wine industry. Beverly W. Goldthwaite is president and general manager and Margaret Shahenian is secretary-treasurer.

At its formation in 1949 the company purchased the brands and listings of the former Alta Winery of Dinuba, Tulare County, where the colorful personality of Charlie Dubbs was for many years the leading light. Soon after Alta bought the Cameo Winery, where it is presently located, along with the Cameo brands and inventories.

Alta Vineyards Company is also the successor to the Mattei name and interests. For many years Andrew Mattei, a native of Switzerland who founded his wine enterprise around 1890 near Malaga, southeast of Fresno, loomed large in the California wine industry and one of Alta's brands still carries his name.

In 1954 a cooperative of grape growers was formed under the name of Cameo Growers, who contracted with Alta for the making and selling of wine from their grapes.

In recent years a gradual merger has taken place between Alta and the Cribari interests in Fresno (see B. Cribari & Sons), so that Alta has become the successor to the former businesses of Alta Winery, Cameo Vineyards Co., A. Mattei and B. Cribari & Sons.

Alta produces and distributes a complete line of table wines, aperitif and dessert wines, vermouths and sparkling wines, marketed under the various *Alta* and *Cribari* brands.

Bisceglia Brothers Wine Co., Fresno

This enterprise was founded in 1888 by four Bisceglia brothers, Joseph, Pasquale, Bruno and Alphonse, who came from a family of vineyardists and wine makers in Cosenza, Province of Calabria, Italy. They first settled in California in the Santa Clara Valley where they went into the wine business and also operated a large cannery. In 1939 the canning operation was discontinued and they directed their full attention to the wine business.

The large and modern winery the Bisceglias are now operating was completed in 1947 and has a capacity of nearly eight million gallons. Standard quality table, sparkling and aperitif and dessert wines are produced and distributed throughout the country.

The last of the original founders, Alphonse F. Bisceglia, passed on in 1952 and the family members now running the enterprise are Bruno T. Bisceglia, president, and Joseph A. Bisceglia, vice president.

Paradise is the leading brand while *Golden Chalice,* introduced in 1953 after years of research, is used for wines of a character all their own, the dessert wines being very sweet.

Cameo Vineyards Company, Fresno
(See **Alta Vineyards Company,** Fresno)

Crest View Winery, Inc., Fresno

The winery was founded in 1935 by John B. Perenchio, who built it. A few years later Joseph Gazzara, the present owner and general manager, purchased part interest in the winery and in 1942 bought the whole of it.

Joseph Gazzara has had long experience in wine making and merchandising. He was born in Italy of a wine growing family, one might say practically in a vineyard. He gained experience in the wine business in his native land, in France, and for many years also in this country. He was already engaged in it before Prohibition and started once more after Repeal, selling sacramental wines during the dry years, as allowed by the laws.

Aperitif or dessert wines are the specialty, while some dry table wines are also available. *Crest View* is the main brand and under that label and its variations, such as *Crest,* sound standard quality wines are produced and marketed nationwide.

B. Cribari & Sons, Fresno

The nationally known house of Cribari was founded in 1904 by Benjamin Cribari and his three sons, Fiore, Angelo and Anthony when Benjamin bought some forty acres in Paradise Valley near Morgan Hill, Santa Clara County, and planted them to vineyards. Later new quarters were established at Madrone on El Camino Real south of San Jose. Here the Cribaris operated for many years, making their wines famous throughout the nation.

The company continued to expand, acquiring a winery and extensive property in Fresno for the production of aperitif and dessert wines. In 1944 the Madrone establishment was sold and the table wine operation was moved to the Evergreen area east of San Jose. It is here that the *Cribari* table wines are still produced but they will not be for long as real estate developments will, alas, obliterate the vineyards.

In 1954 many of the Fresno holdings were sold and a gradual

merger took place between the Cribari enterprises in Fresno and Alta Vineyards Company of Fresno (see there).

Beverly W. Goldthwaite of Alta is general manager of B. Cribari & Sons while some of the younger generation of Cribaris are active in the firm, including Theodore S. (Ted), K. W. (Ken) and A. B. (Al) Cribari.

Table wines, sparkling wines and the usual aperitif and dessert wines are produced under the *Cribari* brands. Familiar also is the *Famiglia Cribari* label under which Vino Rosso, Vino Bianco, Vino Chianti and other Mello Table Wines are marketed.

Roma Wine Company, Fresno

The Roma Wine Company, founded in 1890, was originally located in Lodi. In 1923 it was acquired by the brothers J. Battista and Lorenzo Cella (see Cella Vineyards, Reedley) who expanded the enterprise moving their headquarters to Fresno in 1935 where they had purchased the Santa Lucia Winery. They embarked on a major expansion program to the extent that the Roma Wine Company became the largest and most modern winery of its time in the world. In 1942 Schenley Industries, Inc. acquired Roma Wine Company and all wineries and physical assets of the enterprise and embarked upon a further expansion and modernization program.

Colonel Albert H. Burton is in charge of over-all production of the Roma Wine Company and other Schenley wine production interests. Richard Auerbach is responsible for production control while Roy Mineau is the chief chemist and quality control supervisor and Raul de Soto is in charge of research. Sales and merchandising are handled through CVA Corporation with headquarters in New York City.

The Roma Winery at Fresno has a crushing capacity of 80,000 tons of grapes a season while total storage capacity is over 16,700,000 gallons of wine. The Roma Winery at Kingsburg has an additional capacity of 7,800,000 gallons.

Winery buildings and operating areas cover some fifty-five acres. With minor exceptions all Roma aperitif and dessert wines are produced from grapes grown in the San Joaquin Valley within a radius of sixty miles from the Fresno winery. White grapes represent about 70 per cent of the total volume crushed and include chiefly Muscat of Alexandria, Feher Szagos, Palomino, Malaga and Thompson Seedless, the last two varieties being used principally for the production of brandy and grape concentrates. The most important dark grapes used are: Zinfandel, Petite Sirah, Carignane and Salvador. Grenache grapes are used for the production of Vin Rosé.

Roma produces and markets sound standard quality which are nationally distributed and also exported to various foreign countries including the Orient. *Roma Reserve* is the basic brand with *Roma Estate* and *Roma Select* the two principal variations, conforming to the demands in different parts of the country.

Under the various *Roma* brands the regular types of table wines, aperitif and dessert wines and sparkling wines (bulk fermented) are available as well as berry wines. Varietal table wines include Zinfandel and Grenache Vin Rosé. In addition, bottle fermented Champagne, Pink Champagne and Sparkling Burgundy are marketed under the *Marie Antoinette* and *Tour Eiffel* brands.

Italian type table wines are available under the *Roma Pride of the Vineyard* labeling and include: Vino d'Uva, Vino Rosso, Vino Bianco, Barberone, Burgundy, Chianti and Zinfandel.

Specialty wines comprise "Creme de Roma," a liqueurlike wine with a sherry base and "Rocket" an aperitif wine with natural pure grape flavors added.

Nicholas G. Verry, Inc., Parlier

Located at Parlier some eighteen miles southeast of Fresno this winery is mainly devoted to the production of Retsina, the resin flavored wine which is especially popular with those of Greek origin.

The founder and president of the company, Nicholas Verry, was born in Sparta, Greece, in 1896. He came to this country when he was a boy of ten but has often returned to Europe on visits and business trips. He learned the art of wine making from his brother-in-law, George Solomos, a well known enologist and chemist of Sparta.

Nicholas Verry is assisted in the family enterprise by his wife who bears the noble name of Athena and is secretary-treasurer of the company while their son, John N. Verry, is vice president.

The Verry family first established themselves in the wine business in California in 1933 with a winery in Glendale, moving to their present location in 1942.

Besides Retsina the winery also produces a wine called *Philery* (Quick Love), a light wine, produced in the same manner as Retsina but without the resin flavoring and possessing its own distinctive bouquet and flavor.

Cella Vineyards, Reedley

Some twenty miles east of Fresno, bordering the San Joaquin Valley foothills, lie the vineyards and main winery of the Cellas, a family famous in the California wine industry.

The story behind Cella Vineyards is the story of two brothers, J. Battista Cella and Lorenzo Cella.

The entry into the wine industry of the two brothers in the U.S. goes back to pre-Prohibition days in New York where they were engaged in a wholesale business operating under the name of Cella and Broglio. In the early 1920's J. Battista moved to California to produce wine to be shipped to New York where his brother Lorenzo remained to handle sales. In 1923 they acquired the then small Roma Wine Company located in Lodi, California. This was the beginning of the growth of the company, which then was operated as a partnership until its incorporation in 1932. In 1931 they acquired the old California Wine Association plant in Manteca, in 1934 the Prima Vista plant at Healdsburg, and in 1935 the Santa Lucia Winery in Fresno. With the acquisition of the Santa Lucia Winery they moved their headquarters from Lodi to Fresno. During the period immediately following the repeal of prohibition they embarked on a major expansion program to the extent that the Roma Wine Company became the largest winery in the world, with branches and plants in various cities throughout the country, including New York, Chicago, Los Angeles and San Francisco.

During this time J. Battista Cella concentrated his efforts on the West Coast while Lorenzo Cella headquartered in the East. Their association was continuous until 1942 when they arranged the sale of the company to Schenley Distillers. For a time both remained with the company. J. Battista became a vice president and director of Schenley and chairman of the board of California Vineyard Association, which had administrative control over all Schenley wine holdings. Lorenzo remained in charge of eastern wine sales.

In 1944 they purchased the Rusconi Vineyard located seven miles north of Reedley, California, which consisted of approximately 1,800 acres of vineyard and a small winery. By 1944 Lorenzo had left Roma Wine Company and was actively engaged in the operation of Cella Vineyards. In 1946 J. Battista had also left Roma and together the two brothers started the expansion of their new company. From a capacity of approximately 1,750,000 gallons, the plant has been expanded to approximately twelve million gallons. In 1948 they acquired the Napa Wine Co. at Oakville (Napa County), with a capacity of 1,700,000 gallons. Other vineyards, which had been acquired by J. Battista Cella, were acquired by Cella Vineyards, and with vineyards at Snelling and Reedley the acreage now approximates 4,000 acres.

J. Battista Cella died in 1959 and Lorenzo Cella in 1960. The latter's son, J. B. Cella II, became president of the firm and Mrs. Ebe Cella Turner, daughter of the late J. B. Cella, became executive vice president. The company remains a family owned corporation with members of the J. Battista Cella and Lorenzo Cella families the stockholders.

Today Cella Vineyards specializes in quality bulk wines and are perhaps the largest producers of California grape concentrate. They also market a limited amount of their wines under various brands. *Parma* is the featured brand for table wines, aperitif and dessert wines, including sparkling wines (bulk process), while *Parma di California* is used for Vino Rosso and Vino Bianco. The *Napa Wine Co.* label is reserved for the premium quality wines, including Grenache Rosé and Palomino Pale Sherry. The latter is aged in oak barrels by natural process. "White Mist" is a featured aperitif wine, while other brands used for table wines, sparkling wines, aperitif and dessert wines include *Bravo, Bravo di California* and *Cella Vineyards*.

Cella Vineyards has also become nationally famous for its *Betsy Ross* Grape Juice. This is the only pure grape juice produced from vinifera variety grapes.

TULARE COUNTY

California Growers Wineries, Cutler

This co-operative winery was organized on April 20th 1936 and began operations at their present address on July first of the same year. It is owned and operated by twenty-three growers who have been in the grape industry for many years.

From the beginning, the grower-members have required the personnel at the winery to produce quality wines and grape brandy. Part of the philosophy of California Growers Wineries is that the farming interest of the growers, so important a part of the California and national agricultural picture, should be harmoniously balanced with those of the producer and the merchandiser of California wines.

The officers of California Growers Wineries are the following: A. Setrakian, president; Leonard P. Le Blanc, vice president; D. H. Bonander, secretary; Carl Olsen, treasurer; E. M. Cobb, assistant secretary-treasurer. Nino Munzio is the wine maker and plant superintendent.

California Growers Wineries specialize in the production of sherries, sweet wines of the "dessert" type and grape brandy, the featured brands being *Growers Old Reserve* and *Growers.*

KERN COUNTY

Di Giorgio Wine Company, Di Giorgio

This company is owned by the famed Di Giorgio Fruit Corporation, one of those legendary free enterprise success stories so characteristic of the United States and embracing the fabulous career of the late Joseph Di Giorgio, farmer, grower, entrepreneur extraordinary and founder of the great corporation that bears his name.

Giuseppe (Joe) Di Giorgio, who died in 1951 at the age of 77, rose from lemon packer on his father's small farm at Cefalù in Sicily to the dynamic direction of a multimillion dollar agricultural organization to become, as the press and the trade hailed him: "The Kublai Khan of Kern County" and "The Paul Bunyan of Agriculture."

Young Peppino, as he was called by his family, decided to leave the Sicilian seminary where he was enrolled, to seek his fortune in America. Armed only with a small consignment of his family's lemon crop, the fourteen year old boy landed in New York where he found work with an importer and fruit jobber at $8 a week.

After a few years he moved to Baltimore where he went into the jobbing business for himself. His chief interest at the time was bananas, for which Baltimore was the chief port. He obtained a loan from the Maryland National Bank and acquired his first corporate enterprise, the Monumental Trading Company. At the age of twenty-one he became a director of the bank.

In 1904 Joe Di Giorgio founded the Baltimore Fruit Exchange, cornerstone of the Di Giorgio auction business. In 1911 he purchased the Earl Fruit Company, a long established California shipper, and seven years later acquired some Florida citrus land, forerunners of the vast Di Giorgio holdings in California and Florida.

Not everything went Joe's way. He fought the United Fruit Company, giant of the banana industry, for his share of this profitable business in a running battle that was to last a quarter of a century but the going was rough. On the verge of bankruptcy he saved himself through a bold arrangement whereby he supplied Jamaican growers with Cuban and Mexican bananas so they could fulfill their commitments in the event of loss by hurricane. In return they provided him with the necessary banana bottoms to make shipments to England and other European centers.

The Di Giorgio firm's eminence in produce auctioneering stems from its founder's early perception that the small grower and city jobber who supplies the small retailer both need a free, open and honest market. This led to the company owning a controlling interest in five major U.S. auction companies.

In 1919 Joe Di Giorgio acquired eighteen square miles of farmland in southern San Joaquin Valley, now officially designated as Di Giorgio, California. The land was wrested from the desert with the aid of pumped water, Di Giorgio remarking: "Fruit is nothing but water and labor and more labor and freight."

He foresaw that Prohibition was doomed. In 1932, driving past the Italian Swiss Colony at Asti, Sonoma County, he stopped and decided to get into the business. This he did with such success that when National Distillers bought Italian Swiss Colony (see there) in 1942, Di Giorgio owned it for 37.5%.

Di Giorgio has many other interests including a resort area in Borrego Valley near Palm Springs, the Del Vista Winery at Delano and lumber mill operations in Oregon. While the Del Vista Winery was sold, at a handsome profit, in 1945, the next year a modern winery, with a storage capacity of 9,500,000 gallons was constructed at Di Giorgio, permitting further expansion of bulk wine production.

The senior Di Giorgio had no children of his own but trained his nephews in the operation of the business. Following his death he was succeeded in the presidency by Joseph S. Di Giorgio while the brothers Philip and Joseph A. and another cousin, Robert Di Giorgio, are vice presidents of the giant enterprise, Robert also being president of the Di Giorgio Wine Company.

The corporation's wine program was stepped up with the acquisition in 1956 of the Santa Fe Vintage Company, makers of *Santa Fe* wines. This company's holdings included a bottling plant in Los Angeles and a winery at Kerman, 15 miles west of Fresno. Thus a new operation began for the Di Giorgio interests, bottling wine for sale under its own brands.

Santa Fe operates as a division of the Di Giorgio Wine Company, a wholly owned subsidiary. Wines for bottling are processed at both the Kerman and Di Giorgio wineries under strict quality supervision. With the acquisition of an additional 4½ acres in East Los Angeles a new 75,000 square foot bottling plant and warehouse with the finest modern equipment was constructed in 1957.

More recently the *Padre* and *Vai Bros.* brands were acquired bringing sparkling wines, vermouths and brandy into the Di Giorgio line of bottled goods. These are marketed along with the *Santa Fe* table and aperitif and dessert wines.

Available directly to the public are "The Di Giorgio Family of Fine Wines," the featured brands being *Santa Fe, Padre* and *Vai Bros.*

Under the *Santa Fe* label a full line of the regular types of generic table wines and of aperitif and dessert wines are produced and marketed as well as Berry Wines and "White Bouquet," of the natural flavored aperitif type.

Padre features table wines, aperitif and dessert wines as well as bottle fermented sparkling wines and champagnes while *Vai Bros.* covers much the same ground but with the addition of Vermouths, both Extra Dry White and Sweet, and Brandy.

XIII

SOUTHERN CALIFORNIA REGION

$\mathcal{T}$HIS, THE THIRD of the great wine producing regions of California, covers the southern part of the state, from Los Angeles and San Bernardino counties down south to the Mexican border. Its over-all climate is warm, though less hot than that of the San Joaquin Valley in the great inland valley region. It is especially noted for its dessert wines, while good table wines, notably of the red varieties, and champagnes of quality are also produced.

Southern California consists of a number of separate wine producing districts of which the Cucamonga district in the southwestern tip of San Bernardino County is the best known. It is followed by the city and county of Los Angeles. Ventura County has a single winery in the Ojai Valley.

There are two further districts in the region, the Riverside district in the northwest section of Riverside County adjoining Cucamonga and the Escondido district centering around the city of that name in San Diego County. No wineries of more than local importance are located in the last two districts, although some very good dessert wines are produced there, notably muscatels in the Escondido district, where the Muscat of Alexandria grape attains its highest quality. It was in San Diego County that the Franciscan missionary Padre Junipero Serra planted, according to tradition, the first Mission vines in 1769.

A. *CUCAMONGA DISTRICT*

Cucamonga, one of the few places in California to retain its old Indian name, is said to be derived from "Cucamongabit," meaning "Land of Many Springs." Cucamonga Indians were living in the district when the Spaniards came and built their El Camino Real. In 1839 Don Tiburcio Tapia, who became president of the Ayuntamiento, or City Council, of Los Angeles and the city's first *alcalde,* obtained the Cucamonga grant from the Mexican Government. It is known that Don Tapia also planted grape vines on the ranch.

Cucamonga was the scene of many turbulent events in its early days and its history makes fascinating reading. Gradually it passed from the violent and romantic Wild West stages to an equally romantic but more peaceful era of agriculture and industry. Magnificently situated in the San Bernardino Valley in the extreme southwestern corner of the county of that name, it lies at the foot of the grandiose range of the San Gabriel Mountains with Cucamonga Peak dominating the scene from an altitude of some 8000 feet.

The Cucamonga wine growing district has become increasingly famous over the years. It centers around the town of Cucamonga, straddling Highways 66 and 99 and spreading north to Etiwanda and Alta Loma and south to Ontario, Guasti, and the Riverside County line. It is threatened, however, like many other wine growing areas, by the encroachment of real estate developments.

The Cucamonga district is noted for its red table wines, especially Grignolino, Zinfandel, and Chianti. These should be consumed young, as they mature early, owing to the warm climate in which the grapes are grown. Cucamonga is also well known for its quality champagnes and aperitif and dessert wines, including ports, sherries, and vermouths.

Cucamonga Vineyard Company, Cucamonga

This winery was for many years the headquarters for the production of the familiar *Padre* and *Vai Bros.* brands, now owned and marketed by the Di Giorgio Wine Company of Di Giorgio, Kern County (see there).

The enterprise, formerly the Padre Vineyard Company, is now known as the Cucamonga Vineyard Company. The winery, founded in 1870, was rebuilt by the Vai family in 1909 and enjoys the distinction of being California's Bonded Winery No. 1. The company's main offices are located in Los Angeles. James L. Vai, a legendary figure in the California wine industry who has contributed so much to making Southern California's wines famous, is president. R. Bruce Meeker is secretary-treasurer and Frank Pilone is the wine maker and chemist.

At present the firm concentrates on custom bottling of table wines, aperitif and dessert wines including vermouths, champagnes and other sparkling wines, and brandy. The production personnel is highly experienced and as highly regarded. The premises, situated in the heart of the Cucamonga District, contain the bonded winery No. 1, a fruit distillery, a rectifying plant and a bonded warehouse.

The featured house brand is now *San Gabriel,* formerly marketed by the famed old San Gabriel Winery, no longer in existence. *Sic tempus fugit.*

Cucamonga Winery (Original Cucamonga Winery), Cucamonga

This winery claims to be the original one of the district with the Cucamonga name and has contributed a great deal to make the Cucamonga names famous for its table wines, not only in California but also in the Eastern part of the country. It is mainly owned and operated by the Accomazzo family.

Alfred (Fred) Accomazzo and his brother Eduardo, natives of San Desiderio in the Asti region of Piedmont, Italy, came to

Southern California as young men in 1902. Alfred soon engaged in the wine and liquor business and then established his first Bonded Winery in Glendale, California, in 1916. During Prohibition he turned to the real estate business but with Repeal again became identified with the wine industry, this time permanently.

The Cucamonga Winery was founded in 1933 when Alfred Accomazzo joined forces with several partners to operate a winery in the heart of Cucamonga. Vineyards were acquired and soon extended. With careful attention to the arts of wine growing and wine making the firm produced high quality wines which, when introduced to the Eastern markets, gained immediate recognition and have maintained a growing reputation wherever they have been marketed.

The Accomazzo family owns the majority of the stock in the Cucamonga Winery enterprise. Alfred Accomazzo passed away in 1960 but his son Arthur and Edmund E. (Ed), a son of Eduardo Accomazzo, continue the family tradition while Sam Kurland is also prominent in the firm.

It is interesting to note that some of the Cucamonga Winery's vineyards, running to 850 acres, are irrigated and others are not. While the North Coast Counties' vineyards are non-irrigated and those in the Great Inland Valley Region mostly are, those in Southern California are often mixed. This *Guide* has refrained from indicating whether particular vineyards are irrigated or not in areas where either might be the case because, as the Accomazzos point out, the idea that non-irrigated vineyards produce better grapes in warm climates is not always correct. In extremely dry years or in a succession of dry years non-irrigated vineyards will produce crops of grapes lacking the necessary qualities to make good wines. On the other hand, irrigated vineyards should never be over-irrigated. The answer is the *proper* amount of water, whether vineyards are irrigated or not and that is the responsibility of a good vineyardist or wine grower.

The Cucamonga Winery produces only red and white table wines (and Vermouth) one of the few in the district to do so. All are of premium quality, the reds being more typical of the district. They are mainly distributed in the East and Midwest. The featured brand is *Original Cucamonga Winery,* the slogan "Wines to Remember."

The regular types of generic table wines are available as well as Chianti and Dry Muscat and the following red varietals: Barbera, Grignolino and Zinfandel. *Alfredo* is the brand for Vermouth.

Regina Products Company (Formerly Ellena Brothers), Etiwanda

It was in 1901 that Claudio Ellena, who had come to California from Australia, chose the Cucamonga district at the foothills of the San Gabriel Mountains to establish his vineyards. Here he felt that wines could be produced comparable to the finer ones of Italy, where the Ellenas had been wine growers for many generations. He founded his winery at Etiwanda, a few miles east of Cucamonga. Today his son John B. Ellena carries on the family tradition, producing some of the finest wines of Southern California.

John B. Ellena, president of the company, is assisted by Arless T. Ellena the vice president, Joe Garofalo the wine maker and Peter de Valle the chemist.

Table wines, aperitif and dessert wines, including vermouths and sparkling wines are produced as well as brandy. Wines are marketed in distinctive squat or long necked containers, trade-marks of the house.

Regina is the featured brand with *Etiwanda* a subsidiary label.

Assumption Abbey Winery
(see **Brookside Vineyard Company,** below)

Brookside Vineyard Company, Guasti

The owners of this historic family enterprise are the Bianes, wine growers and wine makers in the district for five generations. Marius Biane, the president of the firm, has been in the wine business of the region continuously for over sixty years.

The firm was originally founded by Théophile Vaché who came from his native island of Oléron in France by way of Cape Horn to California in 1830. Two years later he is said to have engaged in the wine business in Monterey, then still under the Mexican flag. He certainly was one of the pioneers of the California wine industry as in 1849 or even earlier he planted vines south of Hollister in San Benito County in the so-called "Vineyard District" later to become the Valliant Vineyards, now leased by Almadén (see there).

Three nephews of Théophile Vaché the elder came to California to join their uncle: Émile, Théophile the younger and Adolphe. A fourth brother, Alfred, remained in France to operate the family winery and distillery. Émile later returned to his native country as did Théophile the elder but Théophile the younger and Adolphe remained in California. Eventually the family moved to Southern California founding a wholesale business of fine wines and spirits in the heart of downtown Los Angeles. In 1882 the Vaché brothers established themselves as "Wholesale Dealers and Rectifiers and Manufacturers of Native Wines, Brandies, Wine Vinegar, Syrups, Etc.," at Old San Bernardino, leasing the winery which Dr. Benjamin Barton had built some years before. The next year they moved to Redlands Junction, hardly a town at that time, some ten miles southeast of San Bernardino, where they built the Brookside Winery.

A French lad by the name of Marius Biane arrived in 1892 from his native district of Gers in Gascony and soon went to work for the brothers Vaché at Brookside. He fell in love with Marcelline, Adolphe Vaché's daughter, and married her. In due course the Biane family carried on the Vaché tradition of wine making in Redlands, Marius also acquiring vineyards in the Cucamonga district. In 1916 the winery was sold and Marius Biane's sons, Philo and François, went to work for Garrett & Company and later for Fruit Industries Ltd., as the California Wine Association (see there) was known at one time. It was not till 1952 that the Bianes revived their own enterprise by re-establishing the Brookside Vineyard Company at Ontario, moving in 1956 to Guasti at their present location.

The Guasti plant which the Bianes purchased from the California Wine Association, built in 1904, has vast storage cellars with walls of stone, three feet thick. One of the units has an underground space, 20 feet below the surface, 175 feet long by 100 feet wide, used for the storage and aging of wines prior to shipment.

Marius Biane celebrated his 84th birthday in 1959. His son, Philo, is vice president and general manager. The fifth generation of the wine making family is represented by Philo's son, Michael, and by René, the son of François (Frank) Biane who passed away in 1958.

The featured brand for premium wines is *Brookside* and under this label generic table wines and Zinfandel as well as aperitif and dessert wines including dry and sweet vermouth are available. *E. Vaché* and *Pico* are subsidiary brands.

The Brookside Winery has for long been noted for its Altar Wines and in its expansion and promotion of the finer wines was approached by the Benedictine Monks of Assumption Abbey, Richardton, North Dakota, to enter into working arrangements with them whereby it would be possible to start the Benedictines in the wine business in the New World, following their ancient Old World tradition.

This was accomplished and so the **Assumption Abbey Winery** was formed as a D.B.A.* of Brookside Vineyard Company and the *Assumption Abbey* brand was launched.

The Benedictine Monks, one of the oldest orders of the Roman Catholic Church, have been characterized by lives devoted to prayer, study and labor. Though devotion is primary, they exemplify Saint Benedict's Rule that monks "live by the work of their hands." Their 1400 year background in the production of wines and related beverages is known the world over. The wonder and skill of the Benedictine's art in wine making and to uplift the heart of man is now captured in Assumption Abbey wines, carry-

* Doing Business As.

ing on the world respected and centuries old Benedictine tradition.

Abbot Hunkler, who is the Abbot of Assumption Abbey, is now known throughout the Benedictine communities as the "Wine Abbot." His wines, produced by the Bianes at their Brookside Winery in Guasti, enjoy a national distribution, from New York to California and from Louisiana to Minnesota.

Assumption Abbey Altar wines are available to the clergy. Under the same brand they are marketed to the public, including Claret, Burgundy and Zinfandel in the red table wines, Chablis, Sauterne, Haute Sauterne and Rhine in the whites, and Vin Rosé. Aperitif and dessert wines comprise: Pale Dry Sherry, Sherry and Cream Sherry, Port, Tokay, Muscatel, Angelica and Marsala.

Garrett & Company, Inc., Guasti

Two great stories of American wine enterprise are merged here. The one of the Garrett family, established in the industry for a century and a quarter and the other that of Secundo Guasti who founded the Italian Vineyard Company, the town of Guasti in the Cucamonga district and the vineyards which were to become known as the largest in the world.

Garrett & Company was founded in 1835 in the heart of the vineyard country of the South. It was in Medoc, North Carolina, named after the famous wine district in the Bordeaux region of France, that the Garrett brothers established their first vineyards and winery and produced from native Eastern grapes the wine first called "Garrett's Scuppernong" later to become so popular under the name of *"Virginia Dare."*

As the nation expanded and moved West, so did the Garretts. The Southern vineyards were enlarged and company branches opened in the Midwest. In 1911 the Garretts reached the West Coast buying vineyards and a winery in Cucamonga. Two years later more vineyards and wineries were acquired, this time in the Finger Lakes district in Upper New York State. Two further expansions took place when holdings were purchased in 1944 in Ukiah, Mendocino County, for the production of dry table wines and a year later the entire property of the famed Italian Vineyard Company was taken over in Guasti.

Today Garrett & Company controls some 7000 acres of vineyards and three wineries in California and other acreage and wineries in New York and North Carolina. The main offices of the company are located in New York City.

Secundo Guasti was a native of Piedmont, Italy, who came to California by way of Mexico. In or about 1883 he planted his first vineyards in the Cucamonga area, the foundation of an enterprise which he gradually built into the huge Italian Vineyard Company with its 5000 acres of vines. He established a small town for his workers, including houses, a store, a firehouse, a school, a church and an inn. The church is a well-known landmark and a favorite subject for painters because of its Italian style and bells and art objects imported from Italy.

The Italian Vineyard Company flourished until after the death of the founder's son, Secundo Guasti II, in 1932, merging during Prohibition with several other large wineries to form Fruit Industries, Ltd. (now the California Wine Association, see there). Later it operated independently again under Nicola Giulii, the son-in-law of the first Secundo Guasti until the enterprise was acquired by Garrett & Company in 1945.

In spite of its size Garrett & Company has always been a family owned and operated concern. It was actually founded by Dr. Frank Garrett but remained quite small during his lifetime. Paul Garrett, his nephew, is the one who built the enterprise into prominence and was its president for many decades before his death in 1940. Affectionately known as Captain Garrett he became a dominating figure in the American wine industry and was known as the dean of American wine growers.

The third generation of the family now runs the concern. D. B. Weed, the president, and Llewellyn J. Barden, vice president and

Pacific Coast manager with headquarters at Guasti, both married daughters of Paul Garrett. Frank P. Huff is treasurer of the company and also one of the directors. Pat Goodrich is the wine maker at the Guasti winery while Samuel Elder holds the same position at the Cucamonga winery and F. Bricarelli at the Ukiah, Mendocino County plant.

Garrett & Company produces and markets wines that enjoy a national distribution. The principal brand featured is *Garrett's* for the medium priced wines while *Paul Garrett* and *I.V.C.* (continued from the days of the Italian Vineyard Company) are used for the higher priced wines. Table and dessert wines, the familiar *"Virginia Dare"* and the berry wines are all produced in California. Only the sparkling wines are still produced in the East.

B. *THE CITY AND COUNTY OF LOS ANGELES*

Where some five years ago Los Angeles still counted twelve wineries, this number has now decreased to seven. No more, alas, is the old San Gabriel Winery in operation at San Gabriel. The time when Los Angeles led California in wine growing and wine production has long since passed. Real estate developments, freeways and other changes of the times, such is the price one has to pay for progress. Often willingly, let it be said. Where Anaheim once was a German colony devoted to the growing of wines, it is now the home of Disneyland, and what more charming city of illusion for both young and not so young any more could there be?

Of the seven Los Angeles wineries that remain, there is one each at Burbank, Rosemead, Whittier, North Hollywood and San Gabriel while the two others are in Los Angeles proper. One of the latter is the well-known Santa Fe Wine Company, formerly an independent concern, now owned and operated by the Di Giorgio Wine Company of Di Giorgio, Kern County. It is there that one will find the winery and its wines discussed.

With a final tribute to the memory of Jean Louis Vignes and

his famed Aliso Vineyard that once covered over a hundred acres of what is now the heart of downtown Los Angeles and with a bow to the Mission Fathers headed by Fra Junipero Serra who were the first to plant and cultivate grapes along the shores of the Pacific, Part Two of this *Guide* comes to a somewhat reluctant close.

Part Three

XIV

HANDY WINE AND FOOD GUIDE

*W*HAT WINE to serve with a particular dish or at a special occasion? At what temperature will a wine taste the best and give the most value for the money? This and related information is presented chartwise in the following pages.

The how and when of serving wines has been overdone. It has also been underdone. Wines *are* at their best at certain temperatures. Certain wines *do* go better with certain foods. There is no point in denying the facts. After all, coffee tastes better hot than tepid and orange juice is tastiest when cold. The same with wines. Red table wines will give the greatest enjoyment when served at the temperature of the room and white table wines when they are chilled. Lukewarm champagne is to no one's liking and overicing it will kill its natural flavor and bouquet. Stirring champagne with a swizzle stick is idiotic, killing the very bubbles it has cost a fortune and centuries of experience to create. So it is really only sage to observe certain very simple rules.

Suggestions follow for nearly every occasion. Should you not agree with them, you can always suit yourself.

A. *WINE WITH, BEFORE AND AFTER MEALS*

Eleven O'Clock (Elevenses)

with English biscuits or cookies.... Sherry (dry or medium), *Brut* or *Extra Dry* Champagne

Lunch

before lunch..................... Sherry (dry or medium), *Brut* Champagne

with lunch..................... Grenache Rosé, Gamay Rosé or other Rosé; *White table wine:* Semillon (dry or medium), Sauvignon Blanc (dry or medium), Chardonnay, Pinot Blanc, Chenin Blanc, Folle Blanche, White (Johannisberg) Riesling, Traminer, Sylvaner, Grey Riesling

with picnic lunch................ Grenache Rosé, Gamay Rosé or other Rosé

Afternoon Refreshments

with cookies or cake............. Port, Muscat, Sherry (medium or Sweet); *Extra Dry* or *Demi Sec* Champagne; Grenache Rosé, Gamay Rosé or other Rosé

Cocktail Party (6-8 o'clock)

with canapes................... *Brut* or *Extra Dry* Champagne, Sherry (dry, medium or sweet), Port, Muscat, Sweet Vermouth

Cocktail Party (6-10 o'clock or later)

with ham, turkey, cold cuts or cas-
serole dinner.................*Brut* or *Extra Dry* Champagne;
Cabernet Sauvignon, Pinot Noir or
Gamay; Grenache Rosé, Gamay Rosé
or other Rosé

Dinner

before dinner...................*Brut* or *Extra Dry* Champagne; Dry
Sherry or Dry Port

with dinner (one wine, white or
red, depending on the main
course, see B. Specific Dishes).. RED: Cabernet Sauvignon, Pinot
Noir, Gamay, Zinfandel, Barbera,
Grignolino
WHITE: Semillon (dry or medium),
Sauvignon Blanc (dry or medium),
Chardonnay, Pinot Blanc, Pinot
Blanc de Noir, Chenin Blanc, White
(Johannisberg) Riesling, Traminer
or Gewurztraminer, Sylvaner, Grey
Riesling

with dinner (one wine regardless
of dish)......................*Extra Dry* Champagne throughout
with formal dinner (two entrees) If white and red, first the white, then
the red; if two reds, Cabernet Sau-
vignon followed by Pinot Noir

with dinner (one table wine and
one with the dessert)..........Red or white table wine with the
main course
With the dessert: Sweet Semillon,
Sweet Sauvignon Blanc, Chateau
Sauterne, *Demi Sec* or *Sec* Cham-
pagne, Moscato Amabile, Moscato
Spumante, Port, Muscat

after dinner.....................Brandy

Supper (after the theatre)

regardless ....*Brut* or *Extra Dry* Champagne

Nightcap

with a snack.....................A split (¼ bottle) of *Extra Dry* or
Demi Sec Champagne, Port, Muscat,
Sweet Sherry

At any time of Day or Night

with English biscuits or cookies....*Brut* or *Extra Dry* Champagne

B. *WINE WITH SPECIFIC DISHES*

THE DISH   THE SUGGESTIONS

Before the Meal

Canapes or Hors d'Oeuvres........*Brut* or *Extra Dry* Champagne, Dry
Sherry
Caviar or Lumpfish...............*Brut* Champagne

Oysters, Fish and Shellfish

Oysters or Clams.................Chardonnay, Pinot Blanc, White
(Johannisberg) Riesling, Traminer,
Sylvaner, Grey Riesling; *Brut* or
Extra Dry Champagne

Fish or Shellfish, plain (boiled,
broiled, poached)...............Semillon (dry or medium), Sauvignon Blanc (dry or medium), Char-
donnay, Pinot Blanc, Chenin Blanc

(dry), Folle Blanche, White (Johannisberg) Riesling, Traminer, Sylvaner, Grey Riesling, Green Hungarian

Fish or Shellfish, creamed.........Semillon (medium or sweet), Sauvignon Blanc (medium or sweet), Chenin Blanc (sweet)

Soups

Clear Soup.....................Dry Sherry
Creamed Soup..................Medium Dry Sherry

Eggs and Salads

Eggs of any kind................No wine as eggs and wine don't mix
Salads ....No wine as it does not blend with vinegar or lemon

White Meat

Veal, Pork......................Semillon (medium), Sauvignon Blanc (medium), Chenin Blanc (medium); Gamay, Zinfandel; Grenache Rosé, Gamay Rosé or other Rosé

Red Meat

Tournedos, Chateaubriand, Filet
  Mignon, Steak, Roast Beef.......Cabernet Sauvignon
Pot Roast, Stew, Spareribs, Short
  Ribs, Meat Patties..............Gamay, Zinfandel
Beef Burgundy...................Pinot Noir
Steak and Kidney Pie............Cabernet Sauvignon, Zinfandel
Beef Stroganoff.................Gamay, Zinfandel
Lamb ....Zinfandel, Gamay

Ham

Hot or Cold.....................Semillon (medium), Sauvignon
Blanc (medium), Pinot Blanc, Pinot
Blanc de Noir; Grenache Rosé,
Gamay Rosé or other Rosé

Poultry

Chicken (broiled, roasted, fried,
  stewed) ....Red or white table wine.
RED: Cabernet Sauvignon, Zinfandel,
Gamay, Pinot Noir. For *white* table
wine choice see Fish or Shellfish,
plain

Chicken, creamed................White table wine; for choice see Fish
or Shellfish, creamed

Turkey, roasted.................Red or white table wine, red pre-
ferred, see Chicken, broiled
On festive occasions: *Extra Dry*
Champagne or Sparkling Burgundy

Long Island Duckling, Goose......Cabernet Sauvignon, Gamay, Zinfandel, Pinot Noir

Game

Wild Duck, Partridge, Pheasant,
  Quail, Squab, Venison..........Cabernet Sauvignon, Gamay, Pinot
Noir

Rabbit

Tame or Wild....................Cabernet Sauvignon, Gamay, Zinfandel, Pinot Noir

Variety Meats and Frogs' Legs

Sweetbreads, Brains, Frogs' Legs...Semillon (medium or sweet), Sauvignon Blanc (medium or sweet), Chenin Blanc (medium or sweet), Traminer or Gewurztraminer

Kidneys, Heart, Tripe, Liver......Zinfandel, Gamay

Cold Cuts

At lunch, dinner or supper........Grenache Rosé, Gamay Rosé or other Rosé; Semillon (dry), Sauvignon Blanc (dry); Chardonnay, Pinot Blanc, Chenin Blanc (dry), Folle Blanche; White (Johannisberg) Riesling, Traminer, Sylvaner, Grey Riesling, Green Hungarian; Zinfandel, Gamay

Casseroles

Any of these....................Red or white table wine depending on what the casserole is made of

Foreign and Exotic Dishes

Spaghetti, Macaroni, Pizza and other Italian Dishes (Pastas).....Barbera, Grignolino, Charbono, Chianti

Goulash ....Zinfandel

Mexican Dishes.................Lager, Ale or Beer

Curried Dishes..................Lager, Ale or Beer

Indonesian Rijsttafel.............Lager, Ale or Beer

Highly Seasoned Dishes..........Lager, Ale or Beer

Cheese

Assorted Cheeses................Cabernet Sauvignon, Pinot Noir, Port

Welsh Rarebit..................Lager, Ale or Beer

Dessert

Desserts, Fruit and Nuts.......... Semillon (sweet), Sauvignon Blanc (sweet), Chateau (type) Sauternes, Chenin Blanc (sweet), *Demi Sec* or *Sec* Champagne, Moscato Amabile, Moscato Spumante, Port, Muscat.

C. *SPECIAL OCCASIONS*

Wedding Receptions.............. *Brut* or *Extra Dry* Champagne
Christening Receptions............ *Brut* or *Extra Dry* Champagne
Birthdays and other anniversaries,
    men .... *Brut* Champagne
Birthdays and other anniversaries,
    women .... *Extra Dry* Champagne, Pink Champagne (Rosé)
New Year's Eve.................. *Extra Dry* Champagne
As a gift for any occasion.......... A bottle or case of any fine wine
Thanksgiving or Christmas Dinner.. Cabernet Sauvignon, Pinot Noir, *Extra Dry* Champagne, Sparkling Burgundy or Champagne Rouge.

D. *GENERAL SUGGESTIONS*

Storage of Wines

The best place.................... Cellar or closet
The temperature................. About fifty-five degrees
The position.................... Lying down to keep the cork moist
The manner.................... Bins or shelves or wooden cases or cartons stood on edge; diamond shaped bins are the best but simple cartons with dividers will do very nicely.

Serving of Wines

White table wines...............	Cold, as they taste better that way, the sweeter the wine, the colder, but they lose their flavor when over-iced. Two to four hours in the refrigerator is about right.
Red table wines.................	At the temperature of the room
Sparkling wines.................	Cold, but not too cold. Two to four hours in the refrigerator is about right
Rosé table wines................	Same as white table wines (see above)
Sherry, Port, Muscat.............	Same as red table wines (see above)
Should the bottle be opened before serving?	Yes, to let the wine "breathe" and release its bouquet; open white wines one half hour, red wines an hour before serving
When should a wine be decanted?..	In the case of fine table wines and Port wines that have thrown a deposit
What is the best wine to use in cooking?	The best and finest only, as they have the most character and flavor; in the case of table wines use the same wine for cooking as served at table with the dish
Who is served first?.............	The host always, who pours a small amount in his glass to make certain the wine tastes right
Serving white California table wine:	Semillon or Sauvignon Blanc; Chardonnay, Pinot Blanc, Pinot Blanc de Noir, Chenin Blanc, Folle Blanche; White (Johannisberg) Riesling, Traminer or Gewurztraminer, Sylvaner, Grey Riesling

Serving red California table wines: . . Cabernet   Sauvignon,   Zinfandel;
                                        Pinot Noir, Gamay; Barbera, Gri-
                                        gnolino, Charbono
Serving rosé California table wines: . . Grenache Rosé, Gamay Rosé, Caber-
                                        net Rosé, Zinfandel Rosé, Grignolino
                                        Rosé
Serving California Champagne: . . . . *Bottle fermented* champagnes:
                                        Brut before the meal, *Extra Dry* dur-
                                        ing and *Demi Sec* or *Sec* with the
                                        dessert; Pink Champagne for the
                                        ladies
Serving California Sherry: . . . . *flor* or non-*flor Sherry,* but made
                                        from the Palomino grape
Serving California Port: . . . . Tinta (Madeira) Port preferably
Serving California Muscat: . . . . Muscat Frontignan (white) or Black
                                        Muscat (red).

Note: Preference has been given here, as elsewhere in this *Guide,* to
the *varietal* wines as in general they will have the most character, bouquet
and flavor. They are also, both as far as character and as name are concerned, typically and distinctively Californian.

XV

MODERN WINE GLASSES

*T*HERE WAS A TIME, not long ago, when decent American wine glasses were hard to obtain. Americans, so generous in most other instances and inclined to like everything big and large and vast, clung for some unexplained reason to puny wine glasses that could do honor to no wine, let alone the host or hostess. They still cling to them, especially in the restaurants where a proper, generous sized wine glass is a rare thing to behold. Recently, thank goodness, American glass manufacturers have seen the light and fair sized wine glasses are available for the home to those who want them.

Modern usage, led by the French firm of Baccarat, the leader in wine glass ware for some centuries, demands wine glasses that are simple, pleasing, elegant in design and that hold about *twice as much wine as one is likely to serve in them*. They should be clear, easy to hold and without gingerbread.

In general the tulip or bowl shaped glasses are considered the most satisfactory. Their stems should be thin, but not too thin; they should above all hold enough to allow the wine to breathe and to release its bouquet. They should never be hollow stemmed as this makes it difficult to clean them adequately. They should be things of joy to own, to look at with pleasure. They should grace the table and shine or sparkle. They should never be small or puny.

A number of acceptable designs for wine glasses will be found on the following pages. They are suggestions only, adaptable to variations.

1. All purpose table wine
8 ounces

2. Claret or Burgundy
10 ounces

3. White wine
6 ounces

4. Rhine wine
6 ounces

1. All purpose table wine glass

Tulip shaped wine glass suited for any table wine, red, white or rosé, holding 8 ounces. A good all purpose type wine glass so that, owning no other wine glass, one still can be correctly prepared for any occasion.

2. Claret or Burgundy glass

Large tulip shaped wine glass, specially suited for a fine Cabernet Sauvignon or Pinot Noir or for any fine Claret or Red Burgundy. It holds 10 ounces but 12 ounces is also appropriate.

3. White table wine glass

Bowl or tangerine shaped wine glass designed for California white wines such as Semillon and Sauvignon Blanc; Chardonnay, Pinot Blanc, Pinot Blanc de Noir, Chenin Blanc or for any wine of the Sauternes, Graves, Chablis and White Burgundy families. It holds 6 ounces and can also be used as a dessert wine glass for Sweet Semillon, Sweet Sauvignon Blanc or Sweet Sauternes.

4. Rhine wine glass

Tall, curved bowl shaped wine glass specifically suited for any white wine of the rhine wine order such as White or Johannisberg Riesling, Traminer or Gewurztraminer, Sylvaner and Grey Riesling or for any wine, of course, of the Rhine and Moselle families. Contents 6 ounces.

Formerly such rhine wine glasses were green, amber or even rose in color; modern practice requires them to be crystal white.

5. Tulip Champagne glass

Tall tulip shaped champagne glass, holding 10 ounces and conforming to modern good taste. It is an elegant type glass, which has

5. *Tulip Champagne*
10 ounces

6. *Port or Muscat*
4–5 ounces

7. *Sherry or Aperitif*
4–5 ounces

supplanted both the flute shaped champagne glass and the familiar saucer shaped champagne glass that is still to be found in many homes and in most restaurants and nightclubs.

The saucer champagne glass will be with us for years to come as it has become so strongly identified with the serving of champagne or any other sparkling wine. Yet the tall tulip shaped champagne glass is much more elegant, distinctive and better suited for the purpose. It should, of course, never be hollow stemmed (see introduction to this chapter).

6. Port or Muscat glass

This is a typical modern and pleasing dessert wine glass, suited well for Port, Muscat or for any other dessert wine, served either with the dessert or between meals with light refreshments. It holds 4 to 5 ounces and, like any other wine glass, should be about half filled.

7. Sherry or Aperitif glass

The proper Sherry glass is traditionally V shaped and is simple in design, like all modern glasses. It can equally well be used for any wine of the aperitif order and holds 4 to 5 ounces, to be filled half way.

XVI

A LIST OF OUTSTANDING
CALIFORNIA WINES

*T*HIS LIST is arranged according to wine type and alphabetically within the district where the wine is produced. Preference
has been given to the varietal wines as being more typically Californian both in character and name. Vintage wines are indicated
with (V).

While there may possibly be California wines as good as those
listed here the author is certain that there are none better.

Awards received at the yearly State Fair at Sacramento and Los
Angeles Fair are helpful but inconclusive to form an overall picture
as not all wineries send their wines in to be judged and some
never do.

In each category of this selective list certain wines will be finer
than others. Every one is entitled to an opinion but one would
have to be a combination of King Solomon and of a Supreme
Court of Wines to make an exact, graduated classification as to
their relative excellence. A solution is to try them all and to decide
for oneself.

A. CALIFORNIA RED TABLE WINES

Cabernet Sauvignon (The premier claret type wine of California)
    SONOMA COUNTY, Sonoma Valley
        Buena Vista Cabernet Sauvignon

Napa County, Napa Valley
    Beaulieu (B V) Cabernet Sauvignon (V)
    Beaulieu (B V) Georges de Latour Cabernet Sauvignon Private
                Reserve (V)
    Inglenook Cabernet Sauvignon (V)
    Inglenook Cabernet Sauvignon, Older Vintages and Special
                Casks (V)
    Charles Krug Cabernet Sauvignon (V)
    Louis Martini Cabernet Sauvignon (V)
    Louis Martini Cabernet Sauvignon Special Reserve (V)
    Souverain Cellars Cabernet Sauvignon
Santa Clara County, Santa Clara Valley
    Almadén Cabernet Sauvignon
    Gemello Cabernet
    Paul Masson Cabernet Sauvignon
    Martin Ray Cabernet Sauvignon (V)
    Martin Ray Cabernet Sauvignon Mariage
Santa Cruz County
    Hallcrest Cabernet Sauvignon (V)
    Wine by Wheeler (Nicasio Vineyards) Cabernet Sauvignon (V)

Zinfandel (typical California red table wine of better than average qual-
    ity, fruity and zestful)
Sonoma County, Sonoma Valley
    Buena Vista Zinfandel
Napa County, Napa Valley
    Charles Krug Zinfandel
    Louis Martini Mountain Zinfandel (V)
    Souverain Cellars Mountain Zinfandel
Solano County
    Cadenasso Zinfandel
Contra Costa County
    Digardi Zinfandel
Santa Clara County, Santa Clara Valley
    Mirassou Zinfandel
    San Martin Zinfandel
Santa Cruz County
    Wine by Wheeler (Nicasio Vineyards) Zinfandel (V)

SAN LUIS OBISPO COUNTY
    York Mountain Zinfandel
SAN BERNARDINO COUNTY, Cucamonga District
    Assumption Abbey Zinfandel
    Cucamonga Winery Zinfandel

Pinot Noir (the great red burgundy type wine)
SONOMA COUNTY, Sonoma Valley
    Buena Vista Pinot Noir
NAPA COUNTY, Napa Valley
    Beaulieu (B V) Beaumont Pinot Noir (V)
    Inglenook Pinot Noir (V)
    Louis Martini Mountain Pinot Noir (V, available also in Magnums)

ALAMEDA COUNTY, Mission San Jose District
    Weibel Pinot Noir
SANTA CLARA COUNTY, Santa Clara Valley
    Almadén Pinot Noir
    Paul Masson Pinot Noir
    Martin Ray Pinot Noir (V)

Gamay (the Beaujolais type wine)
NAPA COUNTY, Napa Valley
    Inglenook Gamay (V)
    Charles Krug Gamay (V)
CONTRA COSTA COUNTY
    Digardi Mountain Gamay
SANTA CLARA COUNTY, Santa Clara Valley
    Paul Masson Gamay Beaujolais

Barbera (full flavored Italian type wine)
SONOMA COUNTY, Sonoma Valley
    Sebastiani Barbera
NAPA COUNTY, Napa Valley
    Louis Martini Mountain Barbera (V)
SAN BERNARDINO COUNTY, Cucamonga District
    Cucamonga Winery Barbera

Grignolino (light colored red wine of Italian origin, see also Grignolino Rosé)
   NAPA COUNTY, Napa Valley
      Brendel's "Only One" Grignolino
   SOLANA COUNTY, Suisun District
      Cadenasso Grignolino
   SAN BERNARDINO COUNTY, Cucamonga District
      Cucamonga Winery Grignolino
      Garrett's I.V.C. Grignolino

Charbono (Soft Italian type red table wine of Piedmontese origin)
   NAPA COUNTY, Napa Valley
      Inglenook Charbono (V)
   CONTRA COSTA COUNTY
      Digardi Charbono

B. CALIFORNIA WHITE TABLE WINES

Sauvignon Blanc (the more aromatic of the Sauternes type wines)
   ALAMEDA COUNTY, Livermore Valley
      Concannon Sauvignon Blanc (V)
      Wente Bros. Sauvignon Blanc (V)
   NAPA COUNTY, Napa Valley
      Beaulieu (B V) Chateau Beaulieu
      Charles Krug Sweet Sauvignon Blanc
   SANTA CLARA COUNTY, Santa Clara Valley
      Novitiate of Los Gatos Chateau Novitiate

Semillon (fruity and flavorful wine of the Sauternes type)
   ALAMEDA COUNTY, Livermore Valley
      Concannon Dry Semillon
      Cresta Blanca Premier Semillon
      Wente Bros. Dry Semillon
      Wente Bros. Sweet Semillon
   NAPA COUNTY, Napa Valley
      Beaulieu (B V) Dry Sauternes (principally Semillon)

    Charles Krug Sweet Semillon
    Louis Martini Mountain Dry Semillon (V)
SANTA CLARA COUNTY, Santa Clara Valley
    Almadén Dry Semillon
    Paul Masson Semillon
    Paul Masson Chateau Masson (Sweet Semillon)

Chardonnay (the Chablis and White Burgundy type wine)
ALAMEDA COUNTY, Livermore Valley
    Wente Bros. Pinot Chardonnay (V)
NAPA COUNTY, Napa Valley
    Beaulieu (B V) Beaufort Pinot Chardonnay (V)
    Inglenook Pinot Chardonnay (V)
    Mayacamas Chardonnay (V)
SANTA CLARA COUNTY, Santa Clara Valley
    Almadén Pinot Chardonnay
    Paul Masson Pinot Chardonnay
    Martin Ray Chardonnay (V)
SANTA CRUZ COUNTY
    Wine by Wheeler (Nicasio Vineyards) Chardonnay (V)

Pinot Blanc (White Burgundy type wine from the Pinot blanc grape)
ALAMEDA COUNTY, Livermore Valley
    Wente Bros. Pinot Blanc (V)
SANTA CLARA COUNTY, Santa Clara Valley
    Almadén Pinot Blanc
    Novitiate of Los Gatos Pinot Blanc

Chenin Blanc (Vouvray type wine from Chenin blanc or Pineau de la
    Loire grapes)
NAPA COUNTY, Napa Valley
    Inglenook White Pinot (V)
    Charles Krug Chenin Blanc
    Charles Krug White Pinot
    Louis Martini White Pinot (V)
    Mayacamas White Pinot (V)
    Souverain Cellars White Pinot

Folle Blanche (from that grape, a fresh, light luncheon wine)
NAPA COUNTY, Napa Valley
  Louis Martini Folle Blanche (V)

White Riesling or *Johannisberg Riesling* (the premier California wine
  of the Rhine wine order)
SONOMA COUNTY, Sonoma Valley
  White Riesling Johannisberger (V)
NAPA COUNTY, Napa Valley
  Beaulieu (B V) Beauclair Johannisberg Riesling (V)
  Louis Martini Mountain Johannisberg Riesling (V)
  Souverain Cellars Johannisberger Riesling
SANTA CLARA COUNTY, Santa Clara Valley
  Almadén Johannisberg Riesling
  Mirassou White Riesling
SANTA CRUZ COUNTY
  Hallcrest White Riesling (V)
  Wine by Wheeler (Nicasio Vineyards) Johannisberg Riesling (V)

Traminer and *Gewurztraminer* (aromatic wine of the Alsatian type from
  the Traminer grape)
SONOMA COUNTY, Sonoma Valley
  Buena Vista Traminer (V)
NAPA COUNTY, Napa Valley
  Inglenook Traminer (V)
  Charles Krug Traminer
  Louis Martini Mountain Gewurztraminer
SANTA CLARA COUNTY, Santa Clara Valley
  Almadén Traminer

Sylvaner (light wine of the Alsatian order from Franken Riesling grapes)
SONOMA COUNTY, Sonoma Valley
  Buena Vista Sylvaner (V)
NAPA COUNTY, Napa Valley
  Louis Martini Mountain Sylvaner (V)
  Souverain Cellars Sylvaner

SANTA CLARA COUNTY, Santa Clara Valley
    Almadén Sylvaner
    Mirassou Sylvaner

Grey Riesling (light wine from Grey Riesling or Chauché gris grapes)
NAPA COUNTY, Napa Valley
    Charles Krug Grey Riesling
ALAMEDA COUNTY, Livermore Valley
    Wente Bros. Grey Riesling
ALAMEDA COUNTY, Mission San Jose District
    Weibel Grey Riesling
SANTA CLARA COUNTY, Santa Clara Valley
    Almadén Grey Riesling

Malvasia Bianca (light sweet wine from the grape of that name)
SANTA CLARA COUNTY, Santa Clara Valley
    San Martin Malvasia Bianca

C. CALIFORNIA ROSÉ TABLE WINES

Grenache Rosé (from Grenache grapes)
NAPA COUNTY, Napa Valley
    Beaulieu (B V) Grenache Rosé
    Souverain Cellars Grenache Rosé
ALAMEDA COUNTY, Mission San Jose District
    Weibel Grenache Rosé
SANTA CLARA COUNTY, Santa Clara Valley
    Almadén Grenache Rosé
SANTA CRUZ COUNTY
    Wine by Wheeler (Nicasio Vineyards) Grenache Rosé

Gamay Rosé (from Gamay grapes)
NAPA COUNTY, Napa Valley
    Inglenook Navalle Rosé (V)
    Charles Krug Vin Rosé
    Louis Martini Napa Gamay Rosé
    Mayacamas Vineyards Gamay Rosé

ALAMEDA COUNTY, Livermore Valley
    Wente Bros. Vin Rosé

Cabernet Rosé (from Cabernet Sauvignon grapes)
    SONOMA COUNTY, Sonoma Valley
        Buena Vista Rose Brook
    NAPA COUNTY, Napa Valley
        Beaulieu (B V) Beaurosé (from Cabernet Sauvignon, Gamay and
            Mondeuse grapes)
        Mayacamas Vineyards Cabernet Rosé
    ALAMEDA COUNTY, Livermore Valley
        Concannon Cardinal Rosé

Zinfandel Rosé (from Zinfandel grapes)
    NAPA COUNTY, Napa Valley
        Mayacamas Vineyards Zinfandel Rosé

Grignolino Rosé (see also under Grignolino)
    NAPA COUNTY, Napa Valley
        Brendel's "Only One" Grignolino Rosé

D. CALIFORNIA CHAMPAGNES (bottle fermented)

Champagne
    SONOMA COUNTY, Sonoma Valley
        Korbel *Nature, Brut* and *Extra Dry*
    SONOMA COUNTY, Sonoma Valley
        Buena Vista Pinot Chardonnay Champagne
    NAPA COUNTY, Napa Valley
        Beaulieu (B V) *Brut* and *Extra Dry*
        Hanns Kornell Third Generation *Brut*
    ALAMEDA COUNTY, Livermore Valley
        Concannon *Brut* and *Extra Dry*
        Cresta Blanca Champagne and *Brut*
    ALAMEDA COUNTY, Mission San Jose District
        Weibel Pinot Chardonnay *Brut*

SANTA CLARA COUNTY, Santa Clara Valley
 Almadén *Brut* and *Extra Dry*
 Paul Masson *Brut* and *Extra Dry*
 Martin Ray Madame Pinot Champagne (V, Blanc de Noir, from
  Pinot noir grapes) and Champagne de Chardonnay (V)
SANTA CRUZ COUNTY
 Wine by Wheeler (Nicasio Vineyards) Champagne *Nature*

Pink (Rosé) Champagne
SONOMA COUNTY, Russian River Valley
 Korbel Rosé Champagne
NAPA COUNTY, Napa Valley
 Beaulieu (B V) Rosé Champagne (from Pinot noir grapes)
 Hanns Kornell Third Generation Pink Champagne (Rosé)
ALAMEDA COUNTY, Livermore Valley
 Cresta Blanca Pink Champagne
SANTA CLARA COUNTY, Santa Clara Valley
 Almadén Rosé (Pink) Champagne
 Paul Masson Pink Champagne
 Martin Ray Sang de Pinot (V, from first light press of Pinot
  noir grapes)

Red Champagne (Sparkling Burgundy)
SONOMA COUNTY, Russian River Valley
 Korbel Rouge Champagne
NAPA COUNTY, Napa Valley
 Beaulieu (B V) Rouge Champagne
 Hanns Kornell Third Generation Sparkling Burgundy
ALAMEDA COUNTY, Livermore Valley
 Cresta Blanca Sparkling Burgundy
ALAMEDA COUNTY, Mission San Jose District
 Weibel Sparkling Burgundy
SANTA CLARA COUNTY, Santa Clara Valley
 Almadén Sparkling Burgundy
 Paul Masson Red Champagne (Triple Red) and Sparkling Bur-
  gundy (Cuvée Rouge)

E. CALIFORNIA APERITIF and DESSERT WINES

Sherry (Dry, Medium and Sweet)
  SONOMA COUNTY, Sonoma Valley
    Buena Vista Ultra Dry Sherry
  NAPA COUNTY, Napa Valley
    Beaulieu (B V) Cream Sherry
    Louis Martini Pale Dry Sherry
    Souverain Cellars Los Amigos Sherry Sack (dry)
  ALAMEDA COUNTY, Livermore Valley
    Cresta Blanca Dry Watch and Triple Cream Sherries
  ALAMEDA COUNTY, Mission San Jose District
    Weibel Solera *flor* Dry, Medium and Cream Sherries
  SANTA CLARA COUNTY, Santa Clara Valley
    Almadén Solera Cocktail, Golden and Cream Sherries
    Richert & Sons Pale Dry, Club and Triple Cream Sherries
  SAN JOAQUIN COUNTY, Lodi District
    Guild Ceremony "Old San Francisco Brand" Pale Dry and
      Cream Sherries

Port (Ruby, Tawny and Vintage)
  SONOMA COUNTY, Sonoma Valley
    Buena Vista Vintage Port
  NAPA COUNTY, Napa Valley
    Louis Martini Tawny Port
  ALAMEDA COUNTY, Mission San Jose District
    Weibel Solera Port (from Tinta Madeira and other grapes)
  SANTA CLARA COUNTY, Santa Clara Valley
    Almadén Solera Ruby and Tawny Ports
    Novitiate of Los Gatos Port
    Richert & Sons Vintage Tawny, Tinta Madeira and Triple Velvet
      Ports
  SAN JOAQUIN COUNTY, Lodi District
    Guild Ceremony "Old San Francisco Brand" Tawny Port
  MADERA COUNTY
    Ficklin Tinta Port and Special Bottlings of Vintage Ports

Muscat de Frontignan
   ALAMEDA COUNTY, Livermore Valley
      Concannon Muscat de Frontignan
   SANTA CLARA COUNTY, Santa Clara Valley
      Novitiate of Los Gatos Muscat de Frontignan

Black Muscat
   ALAMEDA COUNTY, Mission San Jose District
      Weibel Cream of Black Muscat
   SANTA CLARA COUNTY, Santa Clara Valley
      Novitiate of Los Gatos Black Muscat

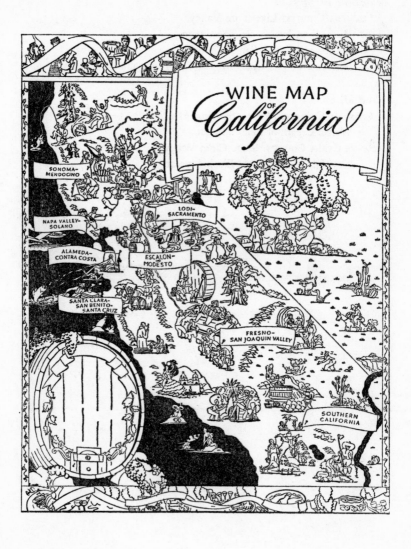

WINE MAP
OF California

SONOMA-
MENDOCINO

NAPA VALLEY-
SOLANO

ALAMEDA-
CONTRA COSTA

SANTA CLARA-
SAN BENITO-
SANTA CRUZ

LODI-
SACRAMENTO

ESCALON-
MODESTO

FRESNO-
SAN JOAQUIN VALLEY

SOUTHERN
CALIFORNIA

XVII

A LIST OF CALIFORNIA WINERIES
OPEN TO THE PUBLIC

Alameda County

HAYWARD
  Paul Rhodes Winery
  1420 Lower Road
  LUcerne 1-7401

LIVERMORE
  Concannon Vineyard
  P. O. Box 432
  HIlltop 7-3760

  Cresta Blanca Wine Company
  P. O. Box 632
  HIlltop 7-3023

  Wente Bros.
  P. O. Box 471
  HIlltop 7-3603

MISSION SAN JOSE
  Weibel Champagne Vineyards
  P. O. Box 95
  OLiver 6-2340

Alameda County (contd.)

PLEASANTON
Garatti Winery
124 St. Johns Street
VIctor 6-5516

Amador County

PLYMOUTH
D'Agostini Winery
Box 48, Aukum Road
CHapel 5-6612

Contra Costa County

MARTINEZ
J. E. Digardi
P. O. Box 88
ACademy 8-2638

Fresno County

FRESNO
Crest View Winery, Inc.
P. O. Box 1423
CLinton 5-0431

Del Rey Cooperative Winery Association
P. O. Box 287
AMherst 4-3441

Golden State Winery
2234 West Dakota Avenue
BAldwin 9-0249

Fresno County (contd.)

FRESNO (contd.)
Antonio Nonini Winery
2640 N. Dickenson Avenue
AMherst 4-7857

Roma Wine Company
P. O. Box 1592
AMherst 4-9671

KERMAN
Di Giorgio Wine Company
5806 North Modoc Avenue
VInewood 6-9515

KINGSBURG
Muscat Cooperative Winery
P. O. Box 5
TWinoaks 6-3065

Roma Wine Company
P. O. Box 216
TWinoaks 7-2984

PARLIER
Mont La Salle Vineyards (Mt. Tivy Winery)
8418 So. Lac Jac
MElrose 8-3544

REEDLEY
Cella Vineyards
MElrose 8-3511

SANGER
Sanger Winery Association
P. O. Box 657
TRinity 5-2505

Kern County

DELANO
> Delano Growers Cooperative Winery
> Route 1, Box 283
> DElano 9756

> A. Perelli-Minetti & Sons
> P. O. Box 817
> McFarland 55

DI GIORGIO
> Di Giorgio Wine Company
> P. O. Box 428
> EMpire 6-7201

EDISON
> Giumarra Vineyards Corporation
> P. O. Box 3
> EDison 3-7251

Los Angeles County

N. HOLLYWOOD
> Vineland Wine Cellar
> 6012 Vineland Avenue
> POplar 3-2234

LOS ANGELES
> San Antonio Winery, Inc.
> 737 Lamar Street
> CApitol 5-5685

> Santa Fe Wine Company
> 2200 S. Saybrook Avenue
> RAymond 3-9792

Los Angeles County (contd.)

SAN GABRIEL
Viotti Winery
8606 E. Elm Avenue
ATlantic 6-7474

WHITTIER
Old Mill Winery
1955 So. Workman Mill Road
OXford 5-0305

Madera County

MADERA
Ficklin Vineyards
30246 Avenue 7½
ORchard 4-2544

Mission Bell Winery
P. O. Box 329
ORchard 4-5634

Yosemite Winery Association
P. O. Box 1139
ORchard 3-3594

Mendocino County

UKIAH
Parducci Wine Cellars
Route 1, Box 572
HOmestead 2-3828

Napa County

CALISTOGA
  Schramsberg Vineyard Company
    (California Champagne Corporation)
  Route 1, Box 228
  WHitehall 2-5552

NAPA
  Mayacamas Vineyards
  1155 Lokoya Road
  BAldwin 4-4030

  Mont La Salle Vineyards
  P. O. Box 420
  BAldwin 6-5566

RUTHERFORD
  Beaulieu Vineyard
  WOodward 3-3214

  Inglenook Vineyard Company
  P. O. Box 269
  WOodward 3-2116

ST. HELENA
  Beringer Bros.
  P. O. Box 111
  WOodward 3-2663

  Leon Brendel
  P. O. Box 122
  WOodward 3-4106

  Freemark Abbey
  P. O. Box 14
  WOodward 3-3426

Napa County (contd.)

Sᴛ. Hᴇʟᴇɴᴀ (contd.)
Hanns Kornell Cellars
P. O. Box 249
WOodward 3-2334

Charles Krug Winery
  (C. Mondavi and Sons)
P. O. Box 191
WOodward 3-2761

Louis M. Martini
P. O. Box 112
WOodward 3-3541

Mont La Salle Vineyards
P. O. Box 311
WOodward 3-2719

Souverain Cellars
P. O. Box 348
WOodward 3-3688

Sutter Home Winery
State Highway 29
WOodward 3-3104

Placer County

Lᴏᴏᴍɪs
Loomis Winery
Route 2, Box 2072
OLiver 2-7208

Sacramento County

ELK GROVE
  Gibson Wine Company
  P. O. Drawer E
  MUrray 5-9594

FLORIN
  James Frasinetti & Sons
  P. O. Box 213
  GArden 8-2421

SACRAMENTO
  Mills Winery
  Route 2, Box 2852
  EMpire 3-2285

San Bernardino County

CUCAMONGA
  Cucamonga Winery
  P. O. Box 696
  YUkon 2-3684

  Garrett & Company, Inc.
  P. O. Box F
  YUkon 6-2731

  Masi Winery
  11837 Foothill Boulevard
  YUkon 2-5145

  E. & J. Gallo Winery
  12281 Arrow Boulevard
  YUkon 2-5177

San Bernardino County (contd.)

CUCAMONGA (contd.)
Thomas Vineyards
P. O. Box 695
YUkon 2-4642

ETIWANDA
Cucamonga Top Winery
12737 Foothill Boulevard
ETiwanda 6616

FONTANA
Louis Cherpin
15567 Valley Boulevard (US 99)
VAlley 2-4103

GUASTI
Garrett & Company, Inc.
YUkon 6-2731

San Diego County

ESCONDIDO
Borra Winery
P. O. Box 546
SHerwood 5-0535

Ferrara Winery
1120 West 15th Street
SHerwood 5-7632

San Joaquin County

ACAMPO
Acampo Winery & Distilleries
P. O. Box 10
ENdicott 9-2746

San Joaquin County (contd.)

ACAMPO (contd.)
    California Wine Association
    Route 1
    ENdicott 9-3677

ESCALON
    Petri Wineries
    P. O. Box 368
    TErrace 8-7361

LOCKEFORD
    Lockeford Winery
    P. O. Box 648
    RAymond 7-5562

LODI
    Alex's Winery
    R.F.D. 2, Box 227
    ENdicott 8-3160

    Bear Creek Vineyard Association
    P. O. Bin 850
    ENdicott 8-0693

    Del Rio Winery
    P. O. Drawer 30
    ENdicott 9-3591

    East-Side Winery
    P. O. Box 440
    ENdicott 9-4768

    Guild Wine Company
    P. O. Box 519
    ENdicott 8-5151

San Joaquin County (contd.)

LODI (contd.)
   Lodi Winery, Inc.
   P. O. Box 188
   ENdicott 8-0179

   Mid-Valley Winery, Inc.
   P. O. Box 670
   ENdicott 8-5126

   Woodbridge Vineyard Association
   Route 2, Box 356
   ENdicott 9-2614

MANTECA
   Sam-Jasper Winery
   Route 1, Box 304
   TAlbot 3-5616

PORT STOCKTON
   Italian Swiss Colony
   P. O. Box 548
   HOward 3-6170

RIPON
   Franzia Brothers Winery
   P. O. Box 697
   TAlbot 9-1311 or 9-1771

San Luis Obispo County

TEMPLETON
   Pesenti Winery
   Vineyard Drive
   TEmpleton 2791

   Rotta Winery
   TEmpleton 2991

Santa Clara County

GILROY
>Bertero Winery
>Route 1, Box 53
>VInewood 2-3032

>Cassa Bros.
>Route 1, Box 59
>Hecker Pass Road
>VInewood 2-3039

LOS GATOS
>Almadén Vineyards
>P. O. Box 906
>ANdrews 9-1312

>Novitiate of Los Gatos
>P. O. Box 127
>ELgato 4-4137

MORGAN HILL
>Richert & Sons, Inc.
>Edmundson Avenue
>MOrgan Hill 9-0685

MOUNTAIN VIEW
>Gemello Winery
>2003 El Camino Real
>WHitecliff 8-7723

SAN JOSE
>Lone Hill Winery, Inc.
>5310 Harwood Road
>ANdrews 9-1841

Santa Clara County (contd.)

SAN JOSE (contd.)
Mirassou Vineyards
Route 3, Box 344
CYpress 3-5913

SAN MARTIN
San Martin Vineyards Company
P. O. Box 53
MUtual 3-2672

SARATOGA
Martin Ray, Inc.*
UNion 7-3205

Paul Masson Vineyards
13150 Saratoga Avenue
ALpine 2-0400

Santa Cruz County

SOQUEL
Nicasio Vineyards *
Nicasio Way
GArden 3-1073

Bargetto's Santa Cruz Winery
3515 N. Main Street, Route 1
GReenwood 5-0918

WATSONVILLE
S. Martinelli & Company
P. O. Box 549, 227 Third Street
PArkway 4-5145

* By appointment only.

Solano County

FAIRFIELD
Cadenasso Winery
Box 606
HArrison 5-5845

SUISUN CITY
Wooden Valley Winery
Route 1, Box 79
HArrison 5-3962

Sonoma County

ASTI
Italian Swiss Colony
P. O. Box 1
TWinbrook 4-2541

CLOVERDALE
Bandiera Wines
155 Cherry Creek Road
TWinbrook 4-5887

GUERNEVILLE
Korbel Winery
Korbel Station
UNion 9-2803

HEALDSBURG
Cambiaso Winery
1141 Grant Avenue
IDlewood 3-1513

OCCIDENTAL
Lemorel Winery
P. O. Box 42
TRinity 4-3677

Sonoma County (contd.)

SANTA ROSA
  Martini & Prati Wines, Inc.
  2191 Laguna Road
  VAlley 3-2404

SONOMA
  Buena Vista Vineyards
  Old Winery Road
  WEbster 8-2424

  Samuele Sebastiani
  P. O. Box 549
  WEbster 8-5532

Tulare County

CUTLER
  California Growers Wineries
  P. O. Box 38
  LAwrence 8-3055

Index

INDEX

Brand names are printed in *italics*.
Bold type indicates pages where main discussion of winery or
wine appears.